Weeds in My Garden

A weed is more than a flower in disguise.
JAMES RUSSELL LOWELL

Weeds in My Garden

*Observations on Some
Misunderstood Plants*

Charles B. Heiser

TIMBER PRESS
Portland · Cambridge

A weed is but an unloved flower!
ELLA WHEELER WILCOX

Published in 2003 by

Timber Press, Inc.
The Haseltine Building
133 s.w. Second Avenue, Suite 450
Portland, Oregon 97204, U.S.A.

Timber Press
2 Station Road
Swavesey
Cambridge CB4 5QJ, U.K.

Printed through Colorcraft Ltd., Hong Kong

Library of Congress Cataloging-in-Publication Data

Heiser, Charles B.
    Weeds in my garden : observations on some misunderstood plants / Charles B. Heiser.
        p. cm.
    Includes bibliographical references (p.   ).
    ISBN 0-88192-562-4
        1. Weeds. 2. Weeds—Identification. I. Title.
    SB611 .H39 2003
    632'.5—dc21

2002072785

Contents

Color plates follow page 96

Preface

WEEDS HAVE LONG held a special place in my affections. They were the first plants with which I became well acquainted. As a student at Washington University in St. Louis during the Second World War, I became interested in botany. Because of gas rationing, trips to the country to see wild plants were rare, so I combed the vacant lots, railroad yards, and dump heaps around St. Louis in order to learn the plants. These plants, of course, were nearly all weeds. Then in 1946, I was employed as an associate botanist at the University of California, Davis. My primary duty was to teach introductory botany and taxonomy, but I was also expected to identify the weeds that were sent to the university by farmers. Thus I soon acquired a good knowledge of the weeds of California. My first really serious study of a plant was of a weed, the common sunflower, and since that time I have also had the opportunity to carry out research with a number of other weedy species. Thus I feel that I have the background to write a book on weeds. There are already lots of books about weeds. Why another one? Because I wanted to write one. Mine will be a little different.

The garden in the title, I should explain, is not really *my* garden but belongs to Indiana University, but I am rather possessive for I have grown plants there longer than any other person. The garden was established as the Botany Experimental Field in 1948 by our chairman, Ralph E. Cleland. In the early years he grew his evening primroses there, Paul Weatherwax grew grasses, and I grew sunflowers and peppers. Since that time a number of other faculty members and graduate students have grown their experimental plants there, some occasionally finding room for a small vegetable garden. The soil is best described as a clay-loam and in one place where there had once been an airstrip it is mostly clay. Before it became our field, most of the area had been part of an old farm so there was already a good seed bank of weeds. Originally the field occupied seven acres, but a new highway took off a corner of it and we lost about two acres. A chain-link fence was placed around the field, and it has provided an excellent habitat for weedy vines, most of which probably came in with birds. Greenhouses and a head house were put there in 1949, and since that time three sheds have been built to serve for storage. Originally, as I recall, the field was completely devoid of trees, but since that time a number have been planted and a few have come in on their own. Thus there are several shady areas as well as open ones available to weeds. The management of the field has varied greatly over the years. In some years fertilizer has been spread over the entire field, and it has been limed several times. The field slopes, and because of our overcultivation in the early years, we had severe erosion in parts of it. As a result we put in three permanent grass strips on the contour and planted the areas most subject to erosion with perennial grasses.

This description of the field—my garden—has been provided to show that we have a number of habitats available for weeds. When I first made my list of weeds I was surprised to find that it numbered more than a hundred. Not all of them, of course, are present in any given year. Some of those present in the early years I have not seen since, and new ones appear from time to time. My list, I find, includes most of the weeds known from Indiana and a large number of those known from eastern North America, some of which are common throughout the United States. Those weeds adapted to very wet soils are not found there. In this book I have chosen to include, with very few exceptions, only those weeds that have occurred in my garden, for I can claim firsthand knowledge of them. At one time or another I have either hoed them out or mowed them off.

Acknowledgments

This book was started in the 1980s and put aside when I became involved with an exciting new research project. It was Dorothy who persuaded me to return to the book—perhaps because I was getting underfoot at home?

To Jack Humbles, Greg Anderson, Marti Crouch, and Melody Schell for encouragement or typing or both.

To Dale Johnson, my editor at Timber Press, who first heard of my plans for this book many years ago and never gave up on it.

To all the people listed in the references, particularly John Gerard and Thomas Johnson.

To Indiana University, who provided "my" garden.

A Weed by Any Other Name…

*What is a weed? A plant whose virtues
have not yet been discovered.*
RALPH WALDO EMERSON (*Fortune of the Republic*, 1878)

EMERSON'S DEFINITION is still widely quoted, but it is more clever than true. Another much quoted definition is that "a weed is a plant out of place," the earliest source for which I know is Willis S. Blatchley in *The Indiana Weed Book* of 1912, although Asa Gray, sometimes called the father of American botany, wrote in 1879 that "even the most useful plants may become weeds if they appear out of their proper place." The *Random House Dictionary* defines weed as: "1. a valueless plant growing wild, esp. one that grows on cultivated ground to the exclusion or injury of the desired crop. 2. any useless, troublesome, or obnoxious plant, esp. one that grows profusely." Other definitions have been proposed, many of which emphasize that a weed is an unwanted, useless or troublesome plant. In 1949 I wrote that a weed is a plant that grows in places in some way disturbed by man (of course, I would now say people) or his domesticated animals. The disturbed places are roadsides, cultivated fields, vacant lots, and other waste places.

17

Herbert Baker wrote in 1965, "a plant is a 'weed,' if, in any specified geographical area, its populations grow entirely or predominantly in situations markedly disturbed by man (without, of course, being deliberately cultivated plants)." He repeated his definition in 1991. Jack Harlan and Jan de Wet, also in 1965, stated, "'Weediness' refers to an adaptive syndrome which permits a species to thrive and become abundant and difficult to eradicate in areas of human disturbance." Thus I think I have adequate support for my definition. Human disturbance is the key word in the definition of a weed whether or not the plant is useless, unwanted, troublesome, abundant, or difficult to eradicate, although sometimes it may be all of these. Many weeds are unattractive plants—they might be described as ugly—but some have truly beautiful flowers. Some plants, in fact, can be called both weeds and wildflowers as the reader will soon learn.

In the dictionary one will find a second entry for *weed* where it is defined as mourning garments, or clothing, and usually used in the plural form. This word has an origin completely separate from the other, and it seems little known today. I asked nine people if they knew a meaning of weeds other than for plants, and eight of them replied no. Of course, most of these people are younger than I—apparently weeds for widows are no longer popular.

There would be no need to define weed if we followed Pamela Jones. In her otherwise delightful little book, *Just Weeds: History, Myths, and Uses*, she wrote, "Lastly and—ideally—I would like to see the word *weed* abolished altogether for being one of the most intolerant, negative words in the English language." I feel it would be a great loss to our language if we gave up the word. What would a new widow wear if she had to give up weeds? No longer could one say that a child is growing like a weed. Not only is it a most useful word in everyday speech, it has become firmly established in literature. I could list well-known quotations about weeds from Shakespeare, Shelley, Tennyson, Whittier, Lowell, Kipling, Sandburg, as well as from a great number of lesser poets.

Characteristics of Weeds

What makes a plant a successful weed? Many weeds produce huge numbers of seeds. A single plant of hedge mustard (*Sisymbrium officinale*), a common weed of the mustard family, may produce a half million seeds. Some weeds have very effective means of seed dispersal, and many weeds have seeds that retain viability for long periods of time. Those of the evening primrose may still germinate after being buried in the soil more than a hundred years. Some of our worst weeds have very efficient means of reproducing vegetatively, usually by roots or underground stems. Horse nettle and bindweed are good examples. However, many weeds neither produce huge numbers of seeds, have no special means of dispersal, do not have long-lived seeds, nor have vegetative reproduction. In fact, many completely wild plants have one or more of these characteristics. In the final analysis, weeds are plants that are physiologically adapted to growing and reproducing in disturbed habitats. Part of their success certainly stems from their great plasticity, their ability to adapt their form and size to the conditions in which they grow, as was pointed out long ago by Asa Gray with credit to a Professor Claypole. Baker (1965, 1991) stated that weeds have a general-purpose genotype that adapts them to a wide range of disturbed environments. Those interested in characteristics of weeds should consult his excellent papers.

The way in which weeds invade gardens makes some people think of them as aggressive plants, but away from disturbed sites they are not, for they seldom if ever compete with the natural vegetation. Weeds have evolved with people and they are usually aggressive only when they compete with our cultivated plants, which, of course, also evolved with us. Some plants are obligate weeds, that is, entirely dependent on human-disturbed areas for their survival, but others may be facultative and exist in both disturbed and natural environments. Thus the definition—a plant out of place—has its merits. Weeds grow in a great variety of disturbed sites. I have often marveled at how some weeds thrive in highly polluted areas of large cities and how a crack in a paved area often provides a home for a weed, a place where one might think there was not enough soil to support any higher life form.

The very aggressive plants that do compete with natural vegetation are today recognized as invasive plants. These are alien plants, often intentionally introduced as ornamentals, that spread naturally (Cronk and Fuller, 1995). This definition is used to make a distinction between weeds and invasive species. The latter, although they often have very attractive flowers or fruits, not only may compete with natural vegetation but at times may wipe it out, hence they are justly condemned. A few plants in my garden that are treated as weeds are invasive. The worst, most certainly, is Japanese honeysuckle, followed closely by wintercreeper. Some of my other weeds are sometimes listed with the invasives but are not particularly aggressive in my garden. I don't think any of the poets have yet been inspired to say anything about invasive species as they have for weeds, and I think that it is unlikely that they will do so.

How Do Weeds Get Around?

How Do Weeds Get Around?

In the youth of Walter Deane, gardens were not hard to weed;
Our plants were too polite to promiscuously seed,
And profanity produce. Foreign weeds grew only then
In ash barrels far remote,—rarities were they to men.
   Shepherd's-purse grew not, I ween,
   In the youth of Walter Deane.
Little Walter on the wharves used to sit from day to day,
Waiting for the ships to bring plants from lands so far away,
Dandelions, buttercups, white weed, chickweed,—all were new,—
With a thousand other things, well known plants to me and you.
   These, remember, were first seen
   Since the youth of Walter Deane.

                                 EDWARD L. RAND, 1900 (Howard, 1973)

Even without any special means of dispersal, weeds often manage to have very extensive ranges. Since nearly half our weeds came from across the Atlantic, we may first inquire as to how they made the journey. Although at times some seeds may cross oceans by natural means—minute seeds carried by wind, some by migrating birds, and some by ocean currents—it seems likely that most of, if not all, our weedy species arrived with human assistance. From the time of Columbus on, and probably even earlier with the Norsemen and others, ships carried seeds of weeds. These early voyages carried seeds of plants for food directly or for planting after arrival. These seeds often had seeds of other plants mixed with them, as is sometimes still true. Some weeds have seeds that mimic those of crop plants in shape, size, and color, so it is difficult even with modern methods to remove all of them from the crop seeds. Plants of trees and shrubs also crossed the ocean, and these may have had soil attached to their roots that likely contained seeds of weeds. Ship's ballast would have been another rich source of weed seeds. The domesticated animals that made the journey to the Americas were an excellent source of seeds—in their fur, in their guts, and in the mud on their feet. The hay brought along to feed them would have often contained seeds.

Once these Old World weeds were established in America, and as is true of the native weeds as well, people were largely responsible for their spread. At first, trails and roads, and much later, railroads provided avenues for their rapid movement. Farm animals, wagons, and people themselves carried the seeds. Mud on boots or shoes is excellent for their transport, as well as clothing. In the days when I wore cuffs on my trousers, I can remember finding a great variety of seeds in them after my return from a field trip. Then, too, as shall be pointed out later, some of the domesticated plants—both crop plants and ornamentals—gave rise to weeds when they reverted to a feral existence. Wherever people went, weeds were sure to follow. Edgar Anderson (1952), who is responsible for much of what I know about weeds, pointed out "that the history of weeds is the history of man."

In Praise of Weeds

Although I shall treat the virtues of the weeds individually later, here I would like to make some general statements about the value of weeds. To do so I call upon the book by Joseph Cocannouer, *Weeds, Guardians of the Soil*, in which it is maintained that weeds improve the soil, for by having roots that go deeper than those of crop plants, they bring up minerals that then can be used by crop plants. Furthermore, weeds make good mother plants and companions to our crop plants; they improve pastures and should be used in rotation with crop plants; they can be used for composting with excellent results. Finally, Cocannouer informs us that weeds are good foods both for humans and wildlife. He also feels that clean cultivation is a sin and that we should follow the example of the Indians by allowing the weeds to remain in our gardens.

Although I agree with some of what Cocannouer says, I do feel that weeds compete with the plants that we deliberately try to grow. They can deprive our cultivated plants of light, water, and minerals, hence some control is often required. Many people, quite naturally, do not appreciate ragweed or poison ivy or unsightly plants growing near their homes. For the most part, however, in vacant lots and other bare areas, weeds provide a ground cover that helps prevent soil erosion and adds organic material to the soil. They certainly do provide food for wildlife, particularly seeds for birds, and often also make nutritious forage or hay for horses and other domesticated animals. Finally, I should mention an important but often overlooked significance. Quite a number of them have served as subjects of scientific studies, elucidating principles that have contributed to the improvement of our crop plants. Examples are provided in the text.

Weed Control

In most garden stores, a large number of chemicals can be purchased to kill weeds. I don't recommend any of them. Weeds should be eliminated by pulling them up by hand or with a hoe. Many years ago I tried to have a lawn of bluegrass (*Poa pratensis*) but because of weeds I soon gave it up and went to *Zoysia*. It crowds out most weeds and also requires less mowing and watering. Of course, it is green only a few months of the year. As I am a botanist, many people would ask me all kinds of questions about plants and their care, many of them about subjects in which I am not a specialist, but once they saw my non-green yard, questions about lawns ceased entirely.

My ideas about weeds in the vegetable garden have also changed over the years. My grandfather was a farmer and he felt that cleanliness was next to godliness as far as the weeds in his fields were concerned, so I learned early that weeds were to be damned. Still today, many if not most people are fixated on having gardens completely free of weeds, but I'm convinced that it may be largely for appearance's sake and not for the welfare of the cultivated plants. I still hoe around the sunflowers, which I study, and other plants in my vegetable garden when they are young, but long ago I found that once they were taller than the weeds it made little difference if further weeding were done. Had I been growing the plants to sell for my livelihood I might have felt differently. Sometimes when the weeds get fairly high I do mow between the rows, but this is for my own convenience because I do my work early in the morning when the dew is heavy, and I don't enjoy having wet shoes, socks, and trouser legs. As the reader may have gathered, this book will have little to say about weed control.

The Weeds

ALL THE WEEDS treated here are flowering plants, and I have arranged them by families. I give a brief description of each family in as nontechnical terms as possible, and I mention some of the plants of the family that have contributed to human welfare. I could have arranged them in some other way, but having been a teacher I can't resist using families for I have always felt that to appreciate the flowering plants it helps to know something about their close relatives. Moreover, if people have some knowledge of the families, they will have a good start on understanding plant classification and it will facilitate plant identification.

For the individual weeds I decided that I could do no better than adopt the treatment of the herbalists and have chosen John Gerard (1545–1612) as my model, rascal though he may have been. He is the best known of the English herbalists, although Agnes Arber, who was probably the foremost authority on the subject, did not think he deserves the fame that he has been accorded. His *Herball, or, Generall Historie of Plantes* appeared in 1597 and was "enlarged and amended" in 1633 by Thomas Johnson. My quotes are from the latter edition. I have preserved his spelling, and I hope the reader has as much fun as I had in figuring out what some of the words are.

I shall start with *The Names* and attempt to explain them, both the common and scientific ones. The latter are usually more easily explained. Every scientific name of a species is a binomial, composed of the genus name and the specific epithet or trivial name. In taxonomic works the scientific name is followed by the name, or an abbreviation of the name, of the person who described the plant. Thus the common sunflower is *Helianthus annuus* L. The L. is for Carl Linnaeus, who named more of our weeds than any other person. This is not surprising, for taxonomists have accepted his work of 1753, *Species Plantarum*, as the starting point for scientific nomenclature because he was the first to use binomials consistently. The scientific names are usually from Greek or Latin and are most frequently based on some characteristic of the plant, although sometimes they are named after a person or geographical region. In the example, *Helianthus* is Greek and translates as sunflower, and *annuus* is Latin and means annual. (At the time it was named it was the only annual species of sunflower known, but since Linnaeus's time several other annual species have been discovered.) Some of Linnaeus's names are not so readily interpreted, however, for he sometimes adopted a name from an ancient writer whose meaning is obscure or unknown, at least to me. The translation of the scientific names given here nearly all come from Fernald (1950) or Bailey (1949), for my high school Latin has been largely forgotten. The translations of the geographical epithets are not given for I think all of them will be obvious.

A plant can have only one correct scientific name, and this name is recognized the world over, at least among botanists. Such is not true of the common, or vernacular, name. A single plant can, and usually does, have many common names, none necessarily more correct than the others. These, of course, vary from country to country in response to the change in language, and they also may vary from region to region of a country, and sometimes within regions as well. Herb Robert (*Geranium robertianum*) has more than a hundred names in England alone, according to Grigson (1955) (my favorites are kiss-me-love-at-the-garden-gate and granny-thread-the-needle.). On the other hand, it is usually impossible to know the person who first gave a common name to the plant and why he did so. One of the common names of the tropical *Galinsoga*, which is usually called quick weed in the United States, is somewhat of an exception. When the plant was first grown at Kew Gardens in England, someone hearing the name *Galinsoga*, to whom it meant nothing, repeated it as gallant soldiers, by which it is still known in England (Salisbury, 1961). Many other common names have equally strange origins. For example, the Jerusalem artichoke (*Helianthus tuberosus*) is neither from Jerusalem nor an artichoke. I find colloquial names fascinating, and I have often wondered how the plant got its name. It is partly for this reason that I decided to write this book, but to try to find an explanation for many common names is frustrating. Many books give the common names but very few say anything about their origins. The exception is Geoffrey Grigson (1955, 1974), who in his two books has provided a great deal of information, particularly for those plants found in England, and I have called upon him for many of the explanations.

Common names have become somewhat standardized in the United States, largely because the regional and state floras have usually adopted the same name. Therefore, for most species I give only one, although for some I give other names if they are still widely used as well as some little-known ones that I find interesting. It would perhaps be desirable if all plants had only one common name in English, but if so it would result in a loss of the richness of our language. Elsewhere, I, along with others, have suggested we use the genus name for new cultivated plants and this might also apply to new weeds. Some people say the scientific name is difficult, but that has not stopped the adoption of a number of them—petunia, zoysia, lespedeza, eucalyptus, and geranium among them—although I should add that some plants now called geranium and lespedeza are no longer placed in *Geranium* or *Lespedeza*.

In the past, common names came from the people; today, if a plant doesn't have one, the taxonomic botanists will often provide it, frequently translating the scientific name. No more, I fear, will we have such wonderful names as spring beauty, Queen Anne's lace, and devil's guts, but more like large-flowered Canada St.-John's-wort and common blue heart-leaved aster. I find nothing appealing in such names. For one thing they are much too long. It was the long Latin phrases used three centuries ago to identify plants that led Linnaeus to adopt the binomial. We would be better off using the scientific name—*Hypericum majus* for the first example I gave, *Aster cordifolius* for the second. Not only are the botanists often coining the common names, they are also coming up with some elaborate rules for their formation and use.

Following *The Names*, I give *The Time and Place*. The time is the blooming period in Indiana, which also applies to much of the central and eastern United States. The place is the plant's region of nativity. Nearly half the species are native to eastern North America, and slightly less than half come from Europe or Eurasia. That so many of the weeds come from those parts of the world is not surprising, for agriculture is older in Europe than in North America and plants there had longer to evolve into weeds. Moreover, the earliest voyagers to America came from Europe. The few remaining species come from tropical America, Asia, Africa, or western North America. From my previous experience with weeds, I had expected that about half of them would have been introduced.

The Description is hardly more than a brief synopsis. Originally, I hadn't intended to include any description at all, but I decided that a short, nontechnical one might be in order. I didn't realize how difficult they would be to write, for I am used to using botanical terms, which are much more precise than plain English but I felt they would be of little use to nonbotanical readers. I only hope that botanists don't read them, for if they do I may lose my license to practice botany. Many readers may want to skip the descriptions in order to get to the more interesting parts. But for those who do read them and find words that are not familiar, I am fairly certain that they can locate them in any good dictionary.

The descriptions may help readers recognize some of the plants, but this book is not intended for plant identification. Then, what is one who wants to identify weeds to do? I have several suggestions. First of all, there are a number of books available for their identification, some of them, supposedly at least, intended for nonbotanists. I find our local public library has two such books, and I imagine that other public libraries around the country will also have some. There is a book on the wildflowers of Indiana (Yatskievych, 2000) that includes nearly all my weeds except for the grasses, sedges, and trees, and keys for their identification as well as color photos. What if the weed isn't in books or can't be identified? In most if not all states, there are county agricultural extension agents whom one may ask. These agents likely will know the more common weeds, but the rare and unusual ones may be unknown to them. One may then turn to universities and colleges. At one time, many of these had botanists who usually would be willing to furnish identifications provided the specimen was adequate. The state agricultural university usually will do this as a public service. Many botanical gardens are also willing to help. One should check with them to see what parts of the plant are needed.

Even better is to learn how to identify plants oneself by using books such as Gleason and Cronquist (1991). Some people do this on their own, but it helps to know a little botany to begin. At one time, most universities offered an introductory botany course that gave the necessary background. Today, however, few universities offer such a course, its having been replaced by a biology course, and even where introductory botany is given, the information basic to plant identification is seldom included. Advanced courses in plant taxonomy are still offered for those with the proper prerequisites, and if one is lucky he or she may find short courses specializing in plant identification at some universities and botanical gardens. After reading this paragraph, the reader will see that, although I have retired from teaching, I am still trying to make people into botanists. After all, botany does afford a good deal of pleasure, if not profit.

Had I intended this to be a book for identification, I would probably have included drawings of each plant. Drawings are often helpful in identification but are not essential. When I taught courses in the subject, I found that in the beginning the students wanted to use illustrations to help identify the plants, but before the semester was over I would find that they depended almost entirely on the written descriptions. The drawings that I have included therefore are for pleasure, and I have again borrowed from Gerard, who in turn often borrowed them from someone else. Although most of the drawings represent the species I treat in the text, in a few places I have used a drawing of a very similar species. The few original drawings were done by Marilyn Rudd, who under the name Marilyn Miller did all of the drawings for the first book I ever wrote. The color photos were all taken by me, and nearly all of them were made at the experimental field, my garden.

Finally, I come to *The Virtues.* I have already mentioned the value of weeds in general, and in the text I deal with those of the individual weeds. Some weeds have many virtues, and very few, even some of the most despised ones, have none at all. A great many plants have been used in medicine, and many still are, and weeds are prominent in this regard. Most people are probably aware that herbal medicine is still widely practiced in many parts of the world but do not realize that millions of people in the United States use plants for medicine at least occasionally. Some people have lost faith in conventional medicine and have adopted various alternative forms, some of which involve herbs, a number of which are weeds. I do not go into any great detail as to how these should be used, for I do not have a license to practice medicine, unlike many botanists of earlier centuries, who took their degree in medicine. There are many books that treat the subject. Again, I would suggest that interested readers check their local public libraries. A word of caution is in order. Before using any of the weeds for medicine one should be certain that the plant is correctly identified.

Of particular interest to me is the large number of introduced plants that were adopted for medicine by the Native Americans (Moerman, 1998). Did the Indians learn of the medicinal use of introduced weeds directly from the European settlers or did they acquire this knowledge on their own? It may be difficult to be certain one way or the other. However, we do know that their medicinal use of the plant was sometimes different from that of the Europeans.

A large number of weeds are used as food. Again I shall not go into great detail, nor (with one exception) do I give recipes. There are a number of books that deal with edible wild plants, one with the delightful title of *Eat the Weeds* (Harris, 1975). One that I recommend highly, although now some years old, is by Merritt Fernald and Alfred Kinsey (1958), revised by Reed Rollins. Kinsey, who is better known for his studies of insects and human sexual behavior, was my colleague at Indiana University during my early years here and was a very fine botanist.* I have tried some weeds for food and a few of them I found quite good. I would certainly hate, however, to be confined to a diet of weeds. For those who do want to try them, the same precaution given for medicinal plants applies, for some weeds can be quite toxic. Also, it is inadvisable to collect plants for food that have been sprayed with herbicides or pesticides.

Several weeds belong to species that are cultivated for food. Some of the weeds are the progenitor of the cultivated plant; others may represent escapes from cultivation that have become weedy, and at times the weed and cultivated plant are not directly related but come from a common progenitor. In all these situations, the weeds may be a valuable source of genes for the improvement of the cultivated plant.

---

*As was his wife, Clara. She led a faculty hiking group to which my wife belonged. About once a year after a hike, I would get a call from Mrs. Kinsey, asking if she could bring a plant to me for identification. I always dreaded these occasions, for if she didn't know the plant, usually I didn't either. Nearly always, if I didn't recognize the plant I would pull down my copy of Deam (1940) and together we almost always came up with a name for it.

Although many weeds are downright ugly, still another virtue of many is that they have very attractive flowers. Some of the same species that are weeds are also cultivated as ornamentals, usually representing selections with larger or more colorful flowers. But a warning is in order: Make sure that you know what you may be in for before transplanting a beautiful weed to your yard or garden—some of them may take over the place.

Some other virtues will be found for several of the weeds, but enough of this high-flown prose. A limerick will bring us back to earth—where the weeds belong.

> *There was an old man of Leeds*
> *Who swallowed a packet of seeds*
> *The silly old ass*
> *Was covered with grass*
> *And you couldn't see his head for the weeds.*
> ANONYMOUS (Van der Zweep, 1982)

Aceraceae Maple Family

Trees with opposite, usually simple leaves; fruits winged.

Box Elder *Acer negundo*

The Names. The leaves of the tree do resemble those of the elder (*Sambucus canadensis*), and box probably comes from the resemblance of the wood to that of box (*Buxus*). *Acer* is the old Latin name for the maple, and *negundo* is from an aboriginal name, according to Fernald (1950), and according to Bailey (1949) is of uncertain origin.

The Time and Place. Late spring. Native to much of the United States and extending to Central America. Box elder trees are usually found along streams.

The Description. Easily identified as a maple by its one-winged, one-seeded fruits and distinguished from other maples by having the leaves divided into three or more leaflets.

The Virtues. Box elder is considered the stepchild among the maples because of its very different leaf and its lack of fine wood and colorful leaves. Nevertheless, it is sometimes deliberately planted, often because of its rapid growth. Some Indians used the bark to make an infusion for an emetic. It may also be tapped for the juice in the spring, for a syrup or sugar, although it is much inferior to the sugar maple (*Acer saccharum*, sugar maple) for this purpose. My children used to delight in collecting the fruits to throw into the air to watch them twirl to the ground. Some people have expressed surprise to find trees included among weeds, but some of them meet my definition.

Amaranthaceae Amaranth Family

Herbs, mostly tropical, with small, densely aggregated flowers lacking petals; sepals and the bracts surrounding them thin, dry, often tan, brown, or red but not green. A number of species are sometimes grown as ornamentals for the colorful flower clusters or leaves, two of the most common being the cockscomb (*Celosia cristata*) and love-lies-bleeding (*Amaranthus caudatus*).

Pigweed *Amaranthus hybridus* and *A. retroflexus*
PLATE 1

The Names. Probably they were eaten by pigs, or possibly because they were common in pig lots. Amaranth is also used as the common name and is gaining acceptance as such. *Amaranthus hybridus* has been called smooth pigweed, and *A. retroflexus*, rough pigweed; both have also been called green pigweed, redroot, and wild beet (although they are not related to the beet, *Beta vulgaris*). *Amaranthus* is from the Greek *amarantos*, meaning unfading because the flowers do not wilt; *hybridus* means hybrid, which the plant is not, and *retroflexus* means reflexed, perhaps pertaining to the bracts surrounding the flowers.

The Time and Place. Late summer. Tropical America.

The Description. Coarse annuals, usually two to six feet tall with large, relatively broad, alternate leaves; seeds very numerous but only one to each flower, small, round and shiny black; stems, at least the lower part, and the root often reddish. The smooth amaranth (*Amaranthus hybridus*) cannot always be readily distinguished from the rough pigweed (*A. retroflexus*) except by technical characters of the sepals and bracts. In my garden, I find that the smooth pigweed generally has more slender and smoother stems than the rough pigweed, and moreover, some of the smooth pigweeds at maturity are dark green or reddish brown whereas the rough pigweed is usually a light green.

The Virtues. These pigweeds may be eaten. The Indians probably ate the seeds at times. Related tropical American species were brought into domestication for their seeds in prehistoric times, and these are being promoted as valuable food plants today because of their excellent protein. Moreover, many species are used as vegetables for their leaves. I recall that these were among the plants that my grandmother included in her spring greens. The Indians also used the plants in medicine. The leaves of the smooth pigweed (*Amaranthus hybridus*) were once used to relieve profuse menstruation among the Cherokee. An ornamental form of this species, cultivated for its red flower clusters, is called prince's feather, which I find rather descriptive. In Ecuador another race of this species, with red or maroon leaves and flowers, known as *sangorache*, is an encouraged weed in that it is not deliberately planted but allowed to persist if it comes up in the garden. It has medicinal uses but perhaps more important, it is used to color the traditional beverage on the Day of the Dead (All Souls' Day). I devoted a whole chapter to it in my little book, *Of Plants and People* (1985). Some years ago I grew it in my garden, where it hybridized with our native race. Some of the hybrid derivatives with reddish leaves and flowers still appear there.

Smooth pigweed is one of the world's worst weeds (Holm et al., 1977) and certainly the prodigious production of seeds of this species helps explain its great success as a weed. When I arrived at Indiana University in 1947 I found a jar of amaranth seeds in the teaching collection. On it was written, "Seeds from one plant ripe at one time—not over half of full crop. 262.3 grams. About 520,000 seeds. At 4 sq. ft. each, these seeds would produce plants to cover 47.8 acres." The smooth amaranth is one of the most common weeds in my garden. I haven't seen the rough pigweed there for several years. Many years ago we also had two other weedy amaranths.

Anacardiaceae Cashew Family

Woody plants, mostly tropical, with alternate leaves; flowers small, usually with five petals. In addition to the cashew (*Anacardium occidentale*), the family includes mango (*Mangifera indica*), pistachio (*Pistacia vera*), and sumacs (various species of *Rhus*).

Smooth Sumac or Scarlet Sumac *Rhus glabra*

The Names. Sumac or sumach is an old Arabian name for an Old World species. Smooth is used to distinguish it primarily from the staghorn or velvet sumac (*Rhus typhina*), which is hairy. Scarlet is because of the leaf color in the fall. *Rhus* is the classical name, and *glabra* is Latin for glabrous, meaning smooth or not hairy.

The Time and Place. Early summer. Native to most of the United States and southern Canada.

The Description. Shrub usually three to six feet tall in my garden (can become a small tree); stalked leaves composed of eleven to thirty-one toothed leaflets; small flowers in terminal, much branched structures; small, dry, one-seeded fruits covered with minute reddish hairs.

The Virtues. Scarlet sumac is one of the first plants to color in the fall, and to me its brilliant red foliage is its chief virtue. Many people use the acid fruits to make a refreshing drink after straining the juice and adding lots of sugar. Cooked, the juice is said to relieve sore throats. The plant was also used medicinally in many ways by the Indians and later by the European immigrants. The leaves were often used for smoking by the Indians, either alone or mixed with tobacco or other herbs. The leaves contain large amounts of tannin and can be used for tanning and dyeing leather. An Old World species has been extensively employed for this purpose. Still another species is an important source of lacquer. A variety of *Rhus glabra* with deeply cut leaflets, as well as other species, are cultivated for their ornamental foliage.

Poison Ivy *Toxicodendron radicans*
PLATE 2

The Names. It is, of course, poisonous, and ivy-like in appearance. *Toxicodendron* means poison tree, and *radicans* means rooting, referring to the roots on the stems. In most of the older works this species is given the name *Rhus radicans.*

The Time and Place. Early summer. Native to eastern North America. In my garden poison ivy is most often found on the fence; the plants also come up frequently in my perennial sunflowers and in my home garden. Fruits and seeds are spread by birds.

The Description. A perennial vine, usually a climber on tree trunks, fences, and the like but when nothing is available it may become a sprawling subshrub; leaves divided into three leaflets of various shapes and sizes; flowers yellowish white or greenish white; fruits white, dry, small, and somewhat berry-like. Some people claim to confuse poison ivy with Virginia creeper (*Parthenocissus quinquefolia*), which may grow in similar places but has five instead of three leaflets. "Leaflets three, let it be" is an old saying to help distinguish poison ivy. I think the leaf of poison ivy is more likely to be confused with that of young box elder (*Acer negundo*).

The Virtues. Even a poisonous weed can have some virtues. Birds eat the thin-walled fruits, and other animals, but not humans, may eat the leaves although I have never seen any doing so. Bees pollinate the plants and their honey is not toxic. The plants were used in American Indian medicine and after its introduction to Europe in the seventeenth century it was so used there. But to many its chief virtue is the attractive coloration of the foliage in the fall. The clusters of fruits have been used, at least once, in Christmas wreaths. I recall a news report some years ago when a company in Texas had so used them, only to have to recall the wreaths when they learned what they had put into them.

I am among those who are not sensitive to the poison so I cannot fully appreciate the sufferings of those who are. The toxicity is caused by a nonvolatile oil so that ordinarily one has to come into contact with the plant to receive the oil. Burning the dried leaves or stems will release the oil, however, and one can suffer severe dermatitis from the smoke. Several people have told me, however, they can suffer from poison ivy simply by getting near a plant even if it is not burned. I used to recommend that people wash thoroughly with a strong laundry soap after being exposed to the plant, but I don't really know if it works. Various other folk remedies have also been recommended. Some claim that eating the young leaves will confer an immunity, but I am not sure how one should do that without the leaves contacting the skin. Moreover, I don't know of any scientific evidence that it will be effective. Some claim that some other plants rubbed on the skin serve to remove the oils. Many other plants, including the jewelweed or touch-me-not (*Impatiens*), have been recommended, but I have no great faith in them either. (The juice of the jewelweed has also been recommended to relieve the sting from contact with the stinging nettle (*Urtica*) but I'm not sure that it's not simply the massage of the skin that is the agent. After all, the stinging sensation shortly disappears by itself.) A number of preparations are now available in drugstores that supposedly help, but I suspect that these are little better than the old folk remedies. My dermatologist agreed and told me that it is difficult for dermatologists to treat inflammation from poison ivy but that fortunately it is self-limiting. He also informed me that there is now an agent that can be applied to the skin before venturing into areas with poison ivy. So what to do about poison ivy? Avoid the plant. If you find it in your garden, eliminate it. Although I don't ordinarily recommend chemical weed killers, I do use them to kill poison ivy plants, which continuously crop up in the garden at home, but I can't use them near my perennial sunflowers at the experimental field because they also kill the sunflowers.

Apiaceae Carrot Family

Nearly all members of the Apiaceae, or Umbelliferae, have broad clusters of many flowers whose stalks arise from the same point on the stem like the rays of an umbrella; small flowers with five separate petals borne on top of the ovary; fruit dry, of two seed-

like structures; rather aromatic herbs with large, alternate, usually deeply divided or dissected leaves with broad, sheathing leaf
bases (petioles). The family provides us with a large number of
economic plants used for food or flavoring, including anise, car-
away, celery, carrot, coriander, dill, fennel, parsley, and parsnip
as well as a few ornamentals. Some deadly poisonous plants, such
as poison hemlock (*Conium maculatum*), the hemlock of antiq-
uity, all parts of which are very poisonous, also belong here.

Goutweed *Aegopodium podagraria*
PLATE 3

The Names. It was once thought to be the cure for gout. Also
called bishop's weed for it was found growing near church ruins,
and herb Gerard after St. Gerard, who was invoked to heal gout.
Aegopodium is from the Greek, translating as goat and little foot,
perhaps from the shape of the leaflets; *podagraria* is a combina-
tion of Greek for foot and chain, and the Latin word for gout.

The Time and Place. Summer. Native to Europe. Escapes from
cultivation are the chief source of the weed elsewhere. Although
goutweed was not found in Indiana in 1950, it is now present in
two counties (Yatskievych, 2000).

The Description. Perennial from creeping rootstocks; leaves
long-stalked and divided into leaflets, generally nine near base
and three above, green or green with white margins; flowers
white, petals frequently with incurved tips; flower clusters without bracts.

The Virtues. Although better known today as an edging plant or
ground cover, for which the form with white-margined leaves is

usually grown, it was originally a medicinal plant used for many ailments. Gerard writes,

> Herbe Gerard with his roots stamped, and laid vpon the members that are troubled or vexed with the gout, swageth the paine, and taketh away the swellings and inflammation thereof, ... It cureth also the Hemor-

Goutweed, *Aegopodium podagraria*, called "*Herba Gerardi*, Herbe Gerard, or Aish-weed" by Gerard

rhoids, if the fundament be bathed with the decoction of
the leaues and roots, and the soft and tender sodden
herbes laid thereon very hot.

The source of the weed in my garden is fairly certain. Some
years ago, Barbara Shalucha of Indiana University's department
of botany introduced it as an ornamental ground cover in the
Junior Gardens next to the experimental field. Then, about
1975, we found it had established itself in the field. She claimed
that she was not responsible, for her plant had white-margined
leaves and ours did not. However, she overlooked the possibility
that our weed could have entered by seed, and that the seeds do
not necessarily breed true in her variegated variety. As a weed, so
far it has not posed any problems, and we have taken no pains to
eliminate it. After all, as Gerard says, "once taken roote, it will
hardly be gotten out againe, ..."

Queen Anne's Lace, Wild Carrot, or Bird's Nest
Daucus carota
PLATE 4

The Names. Wild carrot and bird's nest are easily disposed of—
wild carrot because it belongs to the same species as the domesticated carrot and grows naturally; bird's nest because when the
plant goes to fruit, the rays curl up to produce a structure resembling a small bird's nest. Queen Anne's lace is more difficult. I
had always assumed that it received this name because the deli-
cate white flower clusters could be described as lace-like, and
long ago I heard the story of how once when sewing, Queen Anne
pricked her finger, a drop of blood fell in the flower cluster and
was responsible for the red or purple flower in the center of it—
a good example of the inheritance of an acquired characteristic.

Who was Queen Anne? Most writers consider that it was Anne (1665–1714), queen of Great Britain and Ireland, but could have it been some other royal Anne—Anne Boleyn (1507?–1536), second queen consort of Henry VIII, or Anne of Cleves (1515–1557), fourth queen consort of Henry VIII, for example? I think the last is a good candidate for one of her few accomplishments was that she was proficient in needlework. Silverman (1977) credits it to Anne of Denmark (1574–1619), the wife of James I of England. The name of the plant probably originated in England, but if not, we must also consider Anne of Austria, Anne of Brittany, and Anne of France. There is still another problem. Although I think the lace part of the name is derived from the flowers, Silverman points out that at one time it was the fashion for the Queen and her ladies of the court to adorn their hair with lacy leaves, and indeed the leaves of wild carrot are rather lacy. It is obvious now that we are involved in some very difficult problems. Things become even more unsettling when I consulted Grigson (1955), who states that Queen Anne is a "vague use [of her name] for something associated with the past; though it would be pleasant to suppose this is an older name referring not to the eighteenth century queen, but to the beautiful Queen Anne, Danish wife of James I," but in a later book (1974) writes, "?transferred from the Virgin, or St. Anna, the mother of the Virgin." This is rather disturbing, but more so—perhaps shocking is a better word—is that in both books he identifies Queen Anne's lace as the cow parsley (*Anthriscus sylvestris*), known in America as wild chervil. Our Queen Anne's lace is simply wild carrot in England, thus it appears that the name Queen Anne's lace for the wild carrot may have originated in America. Cow parsley and wild carrot both belong to the same family and are rather similar. I would suggest that the name Queen Anne's lace originated in

England for wild chervil and was transferred to the wild carrot in America. It could be, although perhaps more unlikely, that the name originated independently in America for *Daucus carota*.

I think it is apparent that the problems of Queen Anne's lace need attention. I would suggest it be assigned for a Ph.D. thesis.

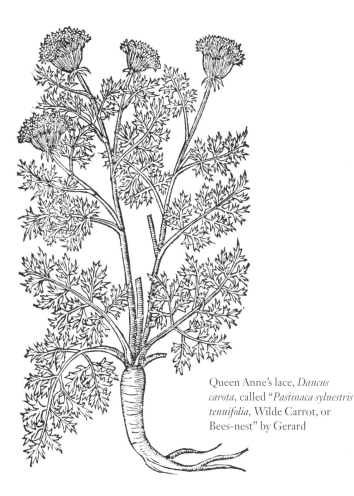

Queen Anne's lace, *Daucus carota*, called "*Pastinaca syluestris tenuifolia*, Wilde Carrot, or Bees-nest" by Gerard

I can see the title now: "The molecular systematics of *Daucus carota* L. and the origin of the name Queen Anne's lace." The major could be in botany and the minors in history and linguistics. The source of the scientific name will come as somewhat of an anticlimax, I'm afraid. *Daucus* is an ancient Greek name for the plant, and *carota* is an old Latin name for carrot.

The Time and Place. Early summer to fall. Gerard tells us that "It groweth of it selfe in vntoyled places, in fields, and in the borders thereof, almost euerie where," and his statement applies to southern Indiana. It is thought to be native to Eurasia, coming to us from Europe and not as an escape from the cultivated carrot.

The Description. Biennial, two to four feet tall, with hairy stems, deeply dissected leaves, and a broad, circular, nearly flat-topped flower cluster; flowers all white or somewhat yellowish, rarely pink, frequently the centermost flower red or purple. Seeds, actually small fruits, somewhat bristly.

The Virtues (and more). Without doubt, Queen Anne's lace is one of the most beautiful of our weeds. If it weren't so common I'm sure it would be intentionally grown. Some people think it too tall, but I think it is about the right height. A field of them can be mowed and in a few weeks one will find lavish blooms on stalks less than half the height of the original. They make good cut flowers, and if a variety of colors is wanted, the stems may be placed in food dyes, as my wife used to do to amuse our daughters.

In some books I have seen it said that one of the virtues of the weed is that it gave rise to the cultivated carrot. The two indeed belong to the same species, but the progenitor was probably rather different from our weed (Banga, 1976). Somewhere I recall seeing the statement that if one saves and plants seeds of the cultivated carrot, after a few years one will end up with the wild carrot. I don't think this will happen unless the plant is grown in the vicinity of wild carrot and hybridization occurs. Where people grow carrots for commercial seed production, they have to be careful that such hybridization doesn't occur.

Opinions are somewhat divided as to the merits of the wild carrot as food. The naturally occurring ones that I have sampled have the distinctive carrot odor, but have always been so spindly and woody that I have been unable to eat them. Therefore, I resolved to plant seed in pots in good garden soil and grow them under ideal conditions. I did so and I am sorry to report that my verdict is the same as before—they are too spindly and woody to serve as food. I learned, however, from Fernald and Kinsey (1958) that a Mrs. Morrell of Maine found that roots raised from seeds were "remarkably sweet." Perhaps there is variation in wild carrot for the edibility of the roots.

At one time the wild carrot was widely appreciated as a medicine. Gerard writes,

> The root boiled and eaten, or boiled with wine, and the decoction drunke, prouoketh vrine, expelleth the stone, bringeth forth the birth; it also procureth bodily lust. The seed drunke bringeth downe the desired sicknesse, it is good for them that can hardly make water, it breaketh and dissolueth winde, it remedieth the dropsie, it cureth the collick and stone, being drunke in wine. It is also good for the passions of the mother, and helpeth conception: it is good against the bitings of all manners of venomous beasts: it is reported, saith *Dioscorides*, that such as haue first taken of it are not hurt by them.

Gerard was not alone in his belief that it provoked bodily lust and for some time it was taken as an aphrodisiac. Today the roots and fruits are still used in herbal medicine, and a tea of either is said to be good for flatulence. The Indians also found some use for it in medicine, although I don't find aphrodisiac or cure for flatulence among them.

Another usage I had not seen mentioned until I read an article in *American Scientist* (Riddle and Estes, 1992) is as a contraceptive. In the Appalachian Mountains of North Carolina some women collect seeds of Queen Anne's lace; then, to prevent pregnancy, before intercourse they drink a glass of water with a teaspoon of the seeds. Seeds are reported to be chewed to reduce fertility in an area of India. These practices were known to women 2000 years ago, and possibly much earlier. Dioscorides, whom Gerard cited, and Hippocrates as well as Galen and a few other ancient physicians were aware of the apparent antifertility activity of the fruits. Several experiments have provided support for their views, although there is some conflicting evidence.

Some additional comments about the red or purple flower in the center of the flower clusters: I was aware that some plants lacked the colorful flower and I had wondered what purpose it might serve. Did it have anything to do with pollination? I thought it unlikely. It turns out that the flower had been the subject of study by Grier (1922). He examined a total of 6148 specimens in two localities and found that only slightly more than one-fourth had it. He tells us that "many botanists have doubtless forgotten Darwin's remarks on the flower of the carrot as given in his work, *Different Forms of Flowers on Plants of the Same Species.*" I had indeed forgotten and had a difficult time finding it, for carrot is not given in the index. Darwin does have a paragraph on it in the introduction. He states, "it cannot be supposed that this one small flower makes the large white umbel at all more conspicuous to insects." He thinks that it is almost certain that the purple flower is of no functional importance to the plant and that it may be a remnant of a former, ancient condition of the species. I am not going to try to improve upon Darwin. From my observations and from the old published account, we can say that a large variety of insects visit the flowers. The same is also true of the cultivated carrot, which has been the subject of more recent studies.

Sanicle or Black Snakeroot *Sanicula canadensis*

The Names. Sanicle comes from the name of the genus. The plant was used by Indians for snakebite. Why black? I don't know but perhaps from the dark green foliage. *Sanicula* is probably from the Latin *santare*, to cure, from a European species used in medicine.

The Time and Place. Summer. Native to eastern North America. Not ordinarily included in weed books, black snakeroot has become a well-established weed in shady areas in my garden in recent years.

The Description. Biennial, two to three feet tall; leaves three- or five-parted, toothed; petals greenish or yellowish; seeds, that is, the fruits, with hooked bristles.

The Virtues. In addition to using it for snakebite, the Indians used it to counter other poisons and treat various ailments. The plants are a nuisance, for if one walks through them, the seeds readily stick to clothing.

Apocynaceae Dogbane Family

Trees, shrubs, woody vines, and herbs with opposite leaves; flowers with five separate petals, twisted in the buds; juice milky. The family includes several plants grown as ornamentals, including periwinkle (*Vinca minor*), oleander (*Nerium oleander*), frangipani (*Plumeria rubra*), and several plants called jasmine but not the true jasmine (*Jasminum* in the olive family, Oleaceae). All parts of oleander are poisonous.

Dogbane, Hemp Dogbane, or Indian Hemp
Apocynum cannabinum

The Names. Bane originally meant death, and later, poison; hence, dogbane means killing dogs or poisonous to dogs. Our plant is known to be toxic to livestock, but the name probably became attached to it from its similarity to the Old World dogbane, a different plant. Hemp is from the use of the fibers, like those of true hemp, *Cannabis sativa* (better known under the name marijuana). *Apocynum* is Greek, *apo*, far from, and *cyon*, dog. The name was used for the Old World dogbane by Dioscorides and transferred to the present genus by Linnaeus, but it is likely that the Old World *apocynum* was a member of the milkweed family (Asclepiadaceae) rather than the dogbane family; *cannibinum* means "like *Cannabis.*"

The Time and Place. Early summer. Native to much of North America. Dogbane was present in my garden many years ago but has long since disappeared.

The Description. Perennial, three to four feet tall with leatherlike bark; leaves pointed, lance-shaped to broadly oval-shaped, long- to short-stalked; petals five, white or greenish white, twisted in the buds; fruits pod-like, slender, about four to six inches long, two to each flower but rarely do all flowers develop fruits; seeds many, each with tufts of long, silky hairs. The presence of a milky juice often leads some to think that dogbane is a kind of milkweed.

The Virtues. Dogbane was a very useful wild plant to the Indians, who used the bark fibers to make twine, bags, fishnets, and a coarse cloth. They also found a great number of uses for it medicinally, including the treatment of heart trouble. It was adopted as a medicine by the European immigrants. Although human deaths have not been reported from ingesting it, dogbane should be considered extremely poisonous. It has been recommended both as a fiber and as a source of natural rubber.

Aristolochiaceae Birthwort Family

Perennial herbs and woody climbers with stalked, alternate, heart-shaped leaves; flowers petal-like, consisting of united sepals (the petals lacking or very small), the flowers usually single in leaf axils. A number of species of tropical aristolochias are grown in greenhouses for their unusual flowers. The wild ginger (*Asarum canadense*), a common late spring wildflower in the eastern United States, belongs to the family. Its spicy rootstock was used as a substitute for ginger by the pioneers.

Pipevine or Woolly Pipevine *Aristolochia tomentosa*
PLATE 5

The Names. The flower is bent somewhat in the shape of a curved pipe and the plant is a vine. *Aristolochia* is from the Greek *aristos*, best, and *lochia*, delivery, from its use in childbirth. The swollen base of the flower was interpreted as a sign from the Creator to suggest its use by pregnant women. The name birthwort is used for the genus. *Tomentosa* is Latin for tomentose, covered with matted hairs, as are the stems and leaves.

The Time and Place. May and June. Native to the southeastern and south-central United States.

The Description. Perennial vine, often climbing high in trees; leaves broad, softly hairy; flowers about one and a half inches long, tubular, curved, with three yellow lobes, and orifice with purple ring; ovary elongate, becoming a capsule about three inches long with many flat seeds.

The Virtues. Pipevine will not be found in any other weed book, for it is hardly a weed, but I include it for it is a most interesting plant and I wanted to write about it. In Indiana it occurs only in a few southwestern counties. On a field trip there about 1960, I saw the plant for the first time and brought seeds home with me.

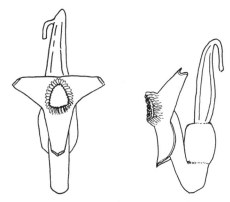

Pipevine, *Aristolochia tomentosa*, flower, drawing by Marilyn Rudd

A half dozen seedlings from these were set around the fence in the experimental field, and they have spread and climbed not only the fence but nearby trees as well. Some of the plants were cut to the ground one year but came up from the roots the next. One of the plants has spread to cover more than a hundred yards along the west fence, completely crowding out and killing my vine of virgin's bower (*Clematis virginiana*)—no great loss, for the pipevine more than adequately serves the same purpose. Only occasionally do the plants produce a seedpod. Although the nearest natural stand of pipevine is only 100 miles away, I think that it is likely that the pollinator, probably a small fly or gnat, does not commonly occur at Bloomington, for only rarely have I found any in the flowers. These may be responsible for the occasional seedpod. I can't say more, for my few attempts at both self- and cross-pollination have failed. The seeds produced are viable, but I do not know whether any have ever germinated and become established at the field.

Flowers of birthworts are trap flowers in that they temporarily imprison insects to bring about pollination. The temperate zone species are not as bizarre as the tropical kinds, one of which may have flowers two feet long and three feet wide. Flowers are often yellow, suffused with purple, so that they resemble decaying meat. They often also have a putrid odor as well and are thus very inviting to carrion flies. When the insects find they were deceived, they try to escape but this is temporarily delayed by one of several methods. Some flowers have a window, a light-colored area near the base of the flower, and the insects try to use it for their escape instead of flying up the dark, curved tubular portion to the opening of the flower. Some species have a very slick tube so that it is difficult for the insects to crawl up. Still others have downward-pointing hairs in the tube that prevent the insect's exit; after pollination the hairs become relaxed so the insect may escape. Some insects, of course, do manage to exit but generally by that time they are covered with pollen. They, however, have not learned their lesson but fly to another nearby flower.

The previous paragraph was written several years ago. In 2001 I was able to learn much more about the flowers and their pollination. I was successful in securing fruits by crossing two different plants, but again my attempts at self-pollination failed to produce any. As a result of this I think that the very low fruit set in earlier years came about because of the inability of the flies, only one to two millimeters long, to fly from one plant to another. In 2001 the two plants that flowered were nearly three hundred yards apart. I examined more than fifty flowers and found insects in over half of them, and a few had as many as five in a single flower. Not all of the insects were successful in their escapes, for I found a few dead ones in some of the flowers. I also learned that the flowers had many of the devices for trapping and imprisoning the flies that I have described: a long tube that may be slippery, and a light-colored band or window just above the basal prison. There are hairs on the prison wall instead of in the tube and these hairs may help delay the escape of the insect until it is covered with pollen. The orifice at the top of the tube is surrounded by a broad, very rough, purple ring that resembles decaying meat. I and several others have never been able to detect any odor to the flowers, but two people have found them to be very malodorous. Whether the flies are rewarded with nectar has yet to be determined.

When I planted the aristolochias in my garden it was with the hope that one day they would provide an interesting problem for a student. It never happened. Now I am trying to entice a former student, Greg Anderson, an authority on flower pollination, to join me in southern Indiana so that we can study the pollination under natural conditions and learn more about the flower's adaptation to fly pollination.

The only other birthwort occurring naturally in Indiana is the Virginia snakeroot (*Aristolochia serpentaria*). Although it is rather common, I find that few people are acquainted with it because it is an inconspicuous little woodland herb with chocolate or purple flowers borne at the base of the plant. In fact, it is not uncommon on the main campus of Indiana University, and I was not aware of it until one of my students, Warren Stoutamire, pointed it out to me some years ago. This plant was once much used in medicine, particularly as a bitter tonic. Deam (1940) wrote, "The fact that the tonic was prepared by adding the roots to whiskey may have added to its popularity."

Asclepiadaceae Milkweed Family

Herbs, shrubs, or vines, usually with a milky juice; leaves opposite, untoothed; flowers of five petals, united at least at the base; fruits pod-like, seeds with a tuft of long, silky hairs. The sexual apparatus of the flower is highly modified, and the pollen, instead of individual grains, is aggregated into pairs of waxy pollen masses attached to each other by arms. (The orchid family has independently evolved aggregation of pollen into masses.) The milkweed family includes a number of ornamentals, chiefly tropical, grown in the greenhouse or outdoors in milder climates. Blood flower (*Asclepias curassavica*), wax plant (*Hoya carnosa*), and the carrion flowers (species of *Stapelia*) belong to this family. The cactus-like nature of *Stapelia* belies its true affinities, for which one must examine the sexual apparatus of the flower.

Milkweed or Silkweed *Asclepias syriaca*
PLATE 6

The Names. This is the most common of the milkweeds and has copious amounts of milky juice. Silkweed comes from the nature of the hairs on the seeds. *Asclepias* is from Aesculapius, the Greco-Roman god of healing; *syriaca* translates as Syrian. Although the plant is American it was early introduced into the Old World, and Linnaeus, who named it, was mistaken in his belief as to its homeland.

The Time and Place. Summer. Native to eastern North America. This milkweed is occasionally naturalized in Europe.

The Description. Perennial, four to five feet tall, all parts softly hairy; leaves large, longer than broad, short-stalked; flowers many, fragrant, in clusters with the stalks coming from a single point; petals five, dull purple; fruits erect, pod-like, with many soft protuberances; seeds many, with tufts of silky hairs.

The Virtues. According to some books, many parts of the plant can be eaten. Young shoots with the hairs removed can be served like asparagus, young leaves can be cooked like spinach, and the cooked young seedpods are supposedly very good. I have seen nothing about eating the young seedpods raw but I had a student, Robert Neher, who ate them and claimed that they had a nut-like taste. I found that he was correct. The dried milky juice can be used as a chewing gum. On the other hand, other books say that it is not wise to eat any parts of the plant for they may contain traces of toxic materials. (But this, of course, is true also of many plants that we eat regularly, such as Irish potatoes and tomatoes.) The Indians, in addition to eating the plants at times, also had a number of medicinal uses for them. During the Second World War the silky hairs were collected to serve as a substitute for kapok in sleeping bags, air jackets, and the like, and it was recommended that the milkweed be cultivated for this purpose.

The entry of milkweeds into my garden can be dated exactly, for none occurred there until 1975 when Susan Kephart introduced them in order to make a study of their pollination for her doctoral degree. She planted several species but all of them disappeared a year or two following the completion of her study except for the common milkweed, one plant of which was still surviving in 2002, and my favorite milkweed, if it should be called that for it doesn't contain a milky juice, *Asclepias tuberosa*, which lasted only a few years. With its very strong yellow, orange, or reddish flowers, *A. tuberosa* is our most attractive milkweed. It is usually called butterfly weed, and the weed part of the name is hardly appropriate. The name pleurisy root is also given to this species, stemming from one of its former medicinal uses.

If a bee or butterfly is found on a milkweed flower and its legs examined closely, it is likely that the waxy, yellowish bags of pollen will be seen. One can extract these from a flower by locating the small, dark, oval glands on the crown of the flower, inserting a pin under one of them, and gently pulling outward. There are five slots on the crown in which the insect will accidentally insert the pollen bag to bring about pollination. In addition to the nectar's serving as food for insects, the common milkweed is also the host plant for the larvae of the monarch butterfly.

Honey Vine, Blue Vine, or Sand Vine *Cynanchum laeve*

The Names. The plant is a vine and is attractive to bees. The leaves might be described as bluish green, which may account for the second name. Sand vine is the translation of its old genus name, *Ampelamus*. The plant may grow in sandy soil, but more often than not it doesn't. *Cynanchum* translates as "to strangle dogs," from a plant that supposedly poisoned dogs (but not necessarily this plant); *laeve* is Latin for smooth, in allusion to the lack of hairs.

The Time and Place. Summer. Native to much of the eastern United States.

The Description. A perennial, twining vine four to six feet tall with broad, heart-shaped leaves; white flowers in clusters; smooth, many-seeded pods, and seeds with silky hairs. Honey vine may be confused with other vines belonging to the milkweed family, such as the common anglepod (*Gonolobus gonocarpos*), which has spreading rather than erect petals, a much shorter crown in the center of the flowers, and is seldom weedy.

The Virtues. Honey vine is a good honey plant and was once recommended for growing by beekeepers. Deam (1940) did this in his home garden, "some seed escaped," and he tried for years to eradicate it without success. He calls it an obnoxious weed but it has caused no problems in my garden.

Asteraceae Aster Family

The Asteraceae, or Compositae as the family is called in older books, is one of the largest families of flowering plants in number of species, next to the orchid family in size worldwide. It has furnished a large number of weeds but in spite of its size has provided us with very few food plants. Lettuce (*Lactuca sativa*) is the best known among the latter, and the sunflower (*Helianthus annuus*) is one of the world's foremost plants in furnishing an edible oil. The family is characterized by having its flowers borne in heads surrounded by bracts. The flowers usually have five petals, united for most of their length. The flowers in the head may all be alike, either tubular or strap-shaped, or the flowers may be of two kinds: the outermost strap-shaped (ray flowers) and the inner ones tubular (disk flowers). When a girl removes the flowers of a daisy to play "he loves me, he loves me not," she picks off the ray flowers one by one. (Boys also play the game, usually with a change of gender in the wording.) The ray flower is not a single petal, contrary to what some might think, but consists of five united petals. The individual seeds in a head are actually one-seeded fruits, known technically as achenes, and they are usually crowned with hairs, scales, or awns—the pappus—which often plays an important role in dispersal. Several members of the family contain a milky juice, and this is indicated in the appropriate places in the following account.

Yarrow or Milfoil *Achillea millefolium*

The Names. Yarrow is from the Anglo-Saxon *gearwe*, whose meaning is not certain. Milfoil means thousand-leaved from the numerous divisions of the leaf. *Achillea* is for Achilles because he is supposed to have discovered its healing properties, and *millefolium*, of course, means thousand-leaved.

The Time and Place. Late spring to early fall. Native to both North America and Europe. Yarrow can be an obnoxious weed but is found only sparingly in my garden.

The Description. Perennial from creeping rootstock, generally one to two feet tall, often somewhat woolly; alternate, usually much dissected leaves, mostly at base of the plant, fewer and smaller above; small heads with short, white (rarely pink) ray flowers and few to many tubular central flowers; aromatic. (Some people consider the odor unpleasant; lacking a better word or nose, I would say it has a medicinal odor.)

Yarrow, *Achillea millefolium*, called "*Achillea, siue Millefolium nobile*, Achilles Yarrow," by Gerard

The Virtues. Yarrow is a rather attractive plant, and not surprisingly, it is also cultivated as an ornamental, as are several other species in the genus. It is fine for dried floral arrangements. Its chief use, however, has been as a medicine both in Europe and North America. Gerard tells us,

> The leaues of Yarrow doe close vp wounds, and keepe them from inflammation, or fiery swelling: it stancheth bloud in any part of the body, and it is likewise put into bathes for women to sit in: it stoppeth the laske, and being drunke it helpeth the bloudy flixe. Most men say that the leaues chewed, and especially greene, are a remedy for the tooth-ache. The leaues being put into the nose, do cause it to bleed, and ease the pain of the megrim.

For a more recent discussion of its medicinal uses, see the article by Chandler et al. (1982) in *Economic Botany.* The genus *Achillea* brings to mind the botanists Jens Clausen, David Keck, and William Hiesey, who used it as one of their subjects in biosystematic studies that had much influence on my own work.

Ragweed *Ambrosia artemisiifolia* and *A. trifida*

The Names. Ragweed is supposedly thus called because of the ragged margin of its leaves. There are two kinds in my garden: common ragweed (*Ambrosia artemisiifolia*) and giant ragweed (*A. trifida*). *Ambrosia* translates as "food of the gods," not very appropriate; *artemisiifolia* means having the leaves of *Artemisia*, wormwood; *trifida* means three-cleft, referring to the leaf.

The Time and Place. Blooming (if it may be called that) in late summer. Native to much of North America. Both species are naturalized in Europe.

The Description. Annuals, leaves opposite below, alternate above; the rayless heads very small and of two kinds: males rather numerous in long spikes and females few and borne in axils of the leaves. Giant ragweed (*Ambrosia trifida*) has unlobed or three- or five-lobed leaves whereas those of the common ragweed (*A. artemisiifolia*) are much divided. The former, as might be expected, is the larger plant, from generally three feet to more than six feet, and the latter usually less than three feet tall.

The Virtues. Ragweed is probably the most notorious plant causing hay fever; it produces copious amounts of wind-blown pollen. The Indians, however, found some virtues in the plant for they used it medicinally in many ways. It has also been speculated that they may have used the fruits for food at times. Fruits of the giant ragweed (*Ambrosia trifida*) have been found in archaeological sites from Indian villages in eastern North America.

Burdock or Clotbur *Arctium minus*

The Names. Bur from the bur-like heads, and dock from its fancied resemblance to that plant (*Rumex*). Clot from an Old English word meaning "to cling," so in a sense clotbur is redundant. Among the many other English names are cockles, cuckold, and love-leaves. *Arctium* comes from the Greek *arctos*, bear, from the rough or bur-like bracts, which have the appearance of the fur of that animal (?); *minus* is Latin for smaller, to distinguish it from the great burdock (*A. lappa*, the epithet meaning bur).

The Time and Place. Summer. From Europe. There are never more than a few in my garden, generally in partially shaded areas.

The Description. Biennial, generally about three feet tall; leaves alternate, the lower quite large and somewhat rounded; flowers pink, tubular, rather inconspicuous; heads about an inch or more across; bracts of the head with a hooked tip that enables the whole structure to function as the bur. Easily distinguished from cocklebur (*Xanthium strumarium*) in that the seeds are many and come out of the head readily.

The Virtues. After peeling away the bitter rind, the stems make a good vegetable. "Surely, when our sophisticated tastes have been trained to favor the burdock, there should be no trouble in eradicating this now obnoxious weed from our yards" (Fernald and Kinsey, 1958). The great burdock (*Arctium lappa*) is cultivated for the food use of its roots in Japan, where it goes under the name *gobo*.

There are many old medicinal uses in Europe for the great burdock, and many of them probably apply to the common burdock (*Arctium minus*) as well, for the two were not considered distinct species until 1800. The root was the part most used. American Indians found many medicinal uses for the common burdock. Burdock is probably the bur mentioned by Shakespeare in several plays.

As far as I am concerned, the burdocks are more objectionable than cocklebur (*Xanthium strumarium*), for I find their burs far more difficult to remove from my clothing and somehow I always manage to rub against the plants in my garden—it's not from affection.

Aster *Aster pilosus*

The Names. The common name obviously comes from the scientific name. Its name is also given as heath aster, awl aster, goodbye-meadow, and frost aster. The last two come from its time of blooming, although it begins earlier than the first frost in

Bloomington. *Aster* comes from the Greek for star, referring to the flower heads; *pilosus* is from the Latin for pilose, referring to the type of hairs, although some plants are not hairy.

The Time and Place. Late summer and fall. Native to eastern North America. It is locally naturalized in Europe.

The Description. Perennial, generally two to three feet tall, usually with moderately hairy stems and leaves; flower heads white, rarely somewhat pink or lavender.

The Virtues. Most of our asters can be considered attractive wildflowers and are particularly desirable for they bloom later than most others. Several species are cultivated as ornamentals, a few of them coming from the Old World. *Aster pilosus*, while perhaps not without some beauty, can be an obnoxious weed but it has never been a problem in my garden. Many of our asters were used in Indian medicine, but this species is not listed.

Spanish Needles, Beggar's-Ticks, and Sticktight *Bidens*

The Names. *Bidens* means two-toothed in reference to the two awns on top of the seed, actually the fruit. Three species occur in my garden: (1) *Bidens bipinnata* (twice pinnate, in reference to the leaves) is called Spanish needles. Needles refers to the narrow, almost needle-like seeds. Spanish is more difficult to explain. The plant is considered native to the eastern United States, but there is a possibility that it came from Latin America, hence Spanish? One dictionary so credits it, but perhaps a more likely origin is because fine needles at one time came from Toledo, Spain. (2) *Bidens frondosa* (leafy, from the outer leaf-like bracts of the head) is known as beggar's-ticks or sticktight in reference to the seeds, which stick to clothing. Tick is a word used in the names of a number of plants whose seed or fruit adheres to clothing, in reference to both the tick-like shape and tendency to cling. (3) *Bidens vulgata* (common) is known by the same names as the other two species.

The Time and Place. Mid- (*Bidens bipinnata*) to late summer. Native to eastern North America; *B. frondosa* and *B. vulgata* native to much of North America. *Bidens bipinnata* and *B. frondosa* are naturalized in Europe.

The Description. Annuals, generally about two to three feet tall with opposite leaves divided into few or many leaflets; heads small to medium size, without ray flowers or these yellow and few and rather inconspicuous; seeds rather flat, with two awns in *Bidens frondosa* and *B. vulgata* or linear-shaped, usually with four awns, in *B. bipinnata*.

The Virtues. These species of *Bidens* are not at all ornamental, but some of the other native species have very showy flowers, although I do not know that they are ever brought into cultivation. One of my students, Gustav Hall, made a study of *Bidens* for his doctoral thesis. Even though the plants he discarded from the greenhouse ended up on a compost heap in my garden, I don't think he deserves the credit (or blame) for introducing these weeds to it, for all three of them are common in the area of Bloomington. In his thesis he pointed out that some of these species have seeds of different shape in the same head and that the different kinds of seed may have different requirements for germination, certainly an advantage for a species in nature. The awns of the seeds of many species have downward-pointing barbs that make them difficult to remove from clothing, as anyone who has rubbed up against a plant knows. This adaptation for dispersal likely came into existence long before people appeared and other animals served as the dispersal agents. Today, of course, people also contribute to the spread of the plant. One of the Latin American species, *B. pilosa*, is a serious weed in the tropics and is one of the world's worst weeds (Holm et al., 1977). It is or was widely used in folk medicine. Surprisingly, little medicinal use is given to our native species, although among the Cherokee, the leaves of Spanish needles were chewed for sore throats and an infusion was taken for worms.

Daisy *Chrysanthemum leucanthemum*
PLATE 7

The Names. The daisy is sometimes called the ox-eye or white daisy or marguerite. Daisy is a contraction of day's eye because the flower head opens in the day and closes at night. Jones (1991) tells us that the name marguerite comes from Margaret of France, who married King Henry VI of England, whereas Grigson (1974) derives it from the French word for the English daisy, which comes from the Latin *margarita* (pearl). The scientific name is one of my favorites to pronounce for it has a certain ring to it. *Chrysanthemum* is from the ancient Greek for golden-flowered; *leucanthemum* is another old Greek name, meaning white-flowered. "White-flowered yellow-flowered" may seem rather inconsistent, but some members of the genus are entirely golden-flowered.

The Time and Place. Early summer. Native to Europe. This daisy is very common in southern Indiana in old pastures and along roadsides but is now rare in my garden.

The Description. Perennial, usually one to three feet tall with alternate, deeply divided or toothed leaves. The large showy head with white rays and yellow disk flowers readily distinguish it from most other weeds.

The Virtues. The beauty of this daisy is its chief virtue. The plant probably spread as a weed from plants that were originally cultivated. Many species of the genus are cultivated as orna-

Daisy, *Chrysanthemum leucanthemum*, called "*Bellis maior*, the great Daisie," by Gerard

mentals. The florists' chrysanthemum (*Chrysanthemum mori-folium*) comes to us from Japan and China, and another species native to Africa (*C. cinerariifolium*) is cultivated for pyrethrum, an insecticide. The daisy (*C. leucanthemum*) was much used for medicine at one time. The ancients dedicated it to Artemis, goddess of females, for it was considered helpful in women's complaints. It was also adopted by the Indians as a medicine, chiefly in the form of a tonic. The plant often called daisy in England is *Bellis perennis*, which is sometimes found as a weed in parts of the United States, including Indiana. *Bellis* is Latin for daisy. The English daisy is a much smaller plant than the ox-eye daisy.

Chicory, Succory, or Blue Sailors *Cichorium intybus*

The Names. Let me deviate from the usual order and begin with the scientific name. *Cichorium* is an altered form of an old Arabian name for the plant. This name traveled through Europe with slight changes and in Middle English became *cicoru*, from which we get *chicory*. Succory may have a similar origin. *Intybus* is another old genus name, probably Latin for chicory.

The Time and Place. Summer. From Eurasia. Chicory is most commonly found along roadsides.

The Description. Perennial from taproot, generally two to three feet tall; leaves toothed to deeply divided, clasping the stem, reduced upward; heads with all ray flowers, showy, blue, very rarely white or pink; juice milky.

The Virtues. Chicory is another weed that is also a cultivated plant, grown for both the leaves and the root. Green or blanched leaves are used for salads but perhaps not as frequently as those of another species, endive (*Cichorium endivia*). Witloof, a name applied to both species and meaning white foliage, comes from the crown of young leaves secured from stored roots. The roots are forced in winter or spring and covered with sand in order to secure white leaves. The young green leaves may also be cooked as a potherb. The roots of chicory are more extensively used than the leaves. They may be eaten raw but more often they are dried, roasted, and ground. They then may be used directly or added to coffee. When I was in New Orleans some years ago I found that there were many coffees in the stores to which chicory had been added. I found the beverage made from them to my liking, particularly as a change from ordinary coffee. I have since learned that one brand of coffee with chicory as well as pure chicory may be purchased locally. It makes an extremely dark brew. The roots are imported from Europe.

Chicory plant was also used medicinally, the root usually being employed, as a tonic, laxative, and diuretic. Medicinal uses by the Indians are also reported. In flower the plants are most attractive. The flower heads are open only in the morning on bright days, however, so the plants are not particularly attractive most of the time. If the flower heads are cut off and placed in water, the blue color fades almost instantly to white.

Thistle *Cirsium vulgare*
PLATE 8

The Names. Thistle is Old English for a prickly plant. This thistle is often called common or bull thistle. *Cirsium* is from the Greek *cirsion*, swollen vein, for which the thistle was once thought to be a remedy; *vulgare* is Latin for common.

The Time and Place. Summer. From Eurasia. Only an occasional plant is found in my garden. According to Deam (1940) this thistle was once common in Indiana and became rare when a butterfly began laying its eggs in the heads and the larvae ate the seed.

The Description. Biennial, usually two to six feet tall, stem spiny-winged, hairy; leaves strongly spiny, deeply divided; heads several, large, with spine-tipped bracts; flowers all tubular, purple.

The Virtues. Peeled, the young tender stalks make a good vegetable. Gerard tells us that thistles in general (according to Galen) "driue forth stinking vrine, if the rootes be boyled in Wine and drunke; and that they take away the ranke smell of the body and arme-holes." The Indians also found medicinal uses for them. A few species of thistle, but not this one, are sometimes grown as ornamentals for bold effects, but perhaps the thistle's greatest claim to fame is that it is associated with the Scottish motto, *Nemo me impune lacessit*, no one attacks me with impunity. The story goes that a foreign raiding party invaded Scotland in ancient times, and the Scots became alerted to their presence from a cry when one of the marauders stepped on a thistle. So we find a thistle as the emblem of Scotland. What species was it? No one knows, but the common thistle is a likely candidate.

> *The rough burr-thistle spreading wide,*
> *Amang the bearded bear,*
> *I turn'd the weeding heuk aside,*
> *An' spar'd the symbol dear.*
>
> ROBERT BURNS

The Canada thistle (*Cirsium arvense*, of the fields), which is not Canadian but comes from Europe, is a far worse weed than the common kind, for it is a perennial from long, spreading rhizomes and reproduces from these as well as from seed. There is a state law in Indiana against having it on one's property, but according to Deam (1940) it was seldom enforced.

Fireweed *Erechtites hieraciifolia*

The Names. The frequent appearance of the plant in burned clearings following a fire is responsible for the common name. (The great willow herb, *Epilobium angustifolium*, of the evening primrose family, is also called fireweed.) *Erechtites* was a name used by Dioscorides; *hieraciifolia* refers to the leaves being like those of a hawkweed (*Hieracium*).

The Time and Place. Late summer. Native to eastern North America.

The Description. Annual, usually two to four feet tall; leaves alternate, oblong to lance-shaped, sharply toothed, to several inches long; heads numerous with whitish tubular flowers; seeds (fruits) topped with many slender, soft, white hairs.

The Virtues. In Asia the tender foliage of fireweed is eaten cooked or raw. The plant was used in American Indian medicine for a variety of purposes and was then adopted as a medicine by European settlers. This weed didn't appear in my garden until 1989 and since that time has occurred in small numbers.

Fleabane *Erigeron annuus* and *Conyza canadensis*

The Names. Bane means poison and these plants, or some very similar plants, were once thought to kill fleas. However, they were also called fleaworts according to one account because the seeds resembled fleas. The annual fleabane (*Erigeron annuus*) is more commonly called daisy fleabane, and indeed the flowers look like small daisies. It is also called white top, which is rather descriptive of the plant but unfortunately of many others as well. The Canada fleabane (*Conyza canadensis*) is also called horse-weed, perhaps because the upper part of the plant resembles a horse's tail or because at times the plant may be the height of a horse. Other names given are hogweed or butterweed, although I have never heard either of them used. *Erigeron* is an ancient Greek name meaning "old man in spring." *Conyza* is another old Greek name for some fleabane; in the older weed books the Canada fleabane is placed in *Erigeron*.

The Time and Place. Annual fleabane (*Erigeron annuus*) blooms in early summer, Canada fleabane (*Conyza canadensis*) in late summer. Both are native to North America and are now found in Europe as weeds.

The Description. Annuals with more or less hairy stems, alternate leaves, and many small heads with white, rarely pink ray flowers and yellow disk flowers. The annual fleabane (*Erigeron annuus*) somewhat resembles an aster but blooms in midsummer whereas our asters don't bloom until late summer or fall. The annual fleabane is generally only two to three feet tall whereas the Canada fleabane (*Conyza canadensis*) is usually taller, sometimes reaching over six feet. Moreover, the latter has smaller heads and much narrower leaves and can be characterized as having an unsightly or bedraggled appearance.

The Virtues. Canada fleabane (*Conyza canadensis*) was used in Indian medicine, particularly for diarrhea. Gerard says that the fleabanes—he lists ten of them—when "burned, where flies, Gnats, fleas, or any venomous things are, doth driue them away."

Several species of *Erigeron* are sometimes grown in the garden as border plants.

White Snakeroot *Eupatorium rugosum*

The Names. Plants called snakeroot have been so named because they were thought to cure snakebites. Some nine different plants from several families have been called snakeroot in the eastern United States. One of these, *Polygala senega,* was used by the Seneca Indians for rattlesnake bites. Although the white snakeroot was used by the Indians for medicine, I do not find that it was used for snakebite. *Eupatorium* comes from Empator, a king of Pontus (an ancient country in Asia Minor), who is reported to have used a *Eupatorium* in medicine; *rugosum* is Latin for wrinkled—not very appropriate.

The Time and Place. Late summer and fall. Native to eastern North America. This snakeroot is found in shady or partially shady places.

The Description. Perennials usually two to four feet tall; leaves opposite, broad, rather thin, regularly toothed; heads many, all the flowers tubular, white.

The Virtues. This rather attractive snakeroot is more often regarded as a wildflower than as a weed. Several species of *Eupatorium,* including this one, are sometimes cultivated for ornament. This one is known to be poisonous to livestock and causes a trembling in animals. When milk from infected cows was drunk by humans it caused "milk sickness" and was responsible for a large number of deaths in the early part of the nineteenth century. Abraham Lincoln's mother is reported to have died from it.

Other eupatoriums were more important than *Eupatorium rugosum* in folk medicine. Three have been used for snakebite. Probably few other American plants were once more widely used than boneset (*E. perfoliatum*) in domestic practice; it was considered a panacea.

Quick Weed *Galinsoga quadriradiata*

The Names. Quick probably because it springs up and flowers rapidly. *Galinsoga* commemorates Mariano Martínez de Galinsoga, founder of the Royal Botanical Garden in Madrid in the eighteenth century; *quadriradiata*, meaning four-radiate, probably refers to the heads' often having four ray flowers. This, or a closely related species, is sometimes called Kew weed in England, for it was introduced to the Royal Botanic Gardens, Kew, and rapidly spread from there (see also p. 27).

The Time and Place. Early to late summer. From tropical America. *Galinsoga quadriradiata* is also a weed in Europe. It comes up in the newly planted ground in my garden every year.

The Description. Annual, seldom over a foot tall, often somewhat sprawling; leaves opposite, broad, and coarsely toothed; heads rather small, with very few white, rarely pink, ray flowers, and yellow, disk flowers.

The Virtues. Few. Young quick weed plants are sometimes cooked as greens in Asia. "If our people take to eating it, the problems of back-yard gardens will be partially solved," according to Fernald and Kinsey (1958). Although quick weed comes up with my annual sunflowers, it is easily hoed out. Deam (1940) calls it a "pernicious weed." A second species, *Galinsoga parvi-*

flora (small-flowered), which also comes to us from tropical America, is also a weed in the United States and is one of the world's worst weeds (Holm et al., 1977).

Sunflower *Helianthus annuus*
PLATE 9

The Names. "The floure of the Sun is called in Latine *Flos Solis*, taking that name from those that haue reported it to turne with the Sun, the which I could neuer obserue, although I haue endeuored to finde out the truth of it; but I rather thinke it was so called because it doth resemble the radiant beames of the Sun, ..." I can add little to Gerard's account except to say that the plant does turn toward the sun until the heads open to display the flowers. *Helianthus* comes from the Greek *helios*, sun, and *anthos*, flower; *annuus*, of course, is Latin for annual, but because there are several other kinds of annual sunflowers, this species is often called the common sunflower. Sunflower, however, when used alone usually refers to this species.

The Time and Place. Mid- to late summer. Native to western North America.

The Description. Annual, usually four to six feet tall; large, alternate, toothed leaves; large heads with showy yellow ray flowers and red or purple disk flowers. Weedy sunflowers are branched and have several heads whereas the sunflower cultivated for food is unbranched and has a single massive head.

The Virtues. Gerard found few virtues for the sunflower, not surprisingly, for it had been introduced to Europe only a few years before he wrote. He does state, however, that "the buds before they be floured, boiled and eaten with butter, vineger, and pepper, after the manner of Artichokes, are exceeding pleasant meat, surpassing the Artichoke far in procuring bodily luste." A later writer, however, found them tasting of turpentine. Why Gerard and other early writers did not try the seeds is surprising, for that was the principal food use of the sunflower among the American Indians. The Indians made medicinal use of the plant but it was the oily seeds, for food, for which it was most highly prized. They domesticated the weed more than three thousand years ago, and the sunflower is the only major food plant other than some of our squashes that was domesticated in what is now the United States. It is now one of the world's major oil crops. The sunflower has also provided us with a number of ornamentals with red or double flowers. Only relatively recently has the sunflower become a popular ornamental in the United States; earlier, it was more appreciated in Europe than in its homeland.

I have been growing the common sunflower in my garden, and many other species as well, for my research every year since 1949, but none of them has become established there as a weed. A few common sunflowers may come up occasionally but they do not persist, although around the outskirts of Indianapolis only sixty miles away they are well established as weeds. One year I left a small plot undisturbed where I had grown my sunflowers the previous year, and the next year sunflowers filled the area—more than a hundred plants. The second year I also found about the same number of plants, but in the third year there were only a dozen plants, and in the next year none at all. I attributed the loss of the sunflowers to weedy grasses that had invaded the area and crowded them out. However, the sunflower has been reported to be allelopathic, that is, the plants produce a toxic substance that inhibits the growth of plants in future years. If this is true, I would have to say that it took a few years for the toxicity to build up to a level that inhibited their growth.

As bird lovers know, birds are fond of sunflower seeds. In my garden every summer not very long after the sunflowers come into flower, goldfinches arrive in great numbers and begin picking the seeds out of the heads long before they are mature. After the seeds mature and the birds land on the plants, some of the mature fruits are shaken to the ground. Goldfinches, I think, are rather inefficient dispersal agents for the sunflower, and very expensive in terms of the numbers of seed they eat. Once on the ground, the seeds are eaten or the fruits are carried away by other animals, field mice, for example. For a plant with such inefficient seed dispersal, the sunflower has a surprisingly large distribution. People, of course, are probably responsible for the extensive distribution of weedy sunflowers today with their automobiles, farm machinery, trains, and the like.

I have written a little book about sunflowers (Heiser, 1976), and for the reader who wants to know more about this most interesting (to me, at least) plant I would suggest consulting it. One thing not in the book is that the sunflower was a candidate for the national flower of the United States. I thought that it would have made a good choice for it is a native, very conspicuous, and not unattractive plant that is found in nearly all parts of the country. Moreover, it contributed much to our country, and as mentioned, was domesticated in the United States. On the other had, some farmers condemn the plant for it is an objectionable weed in many places, and some people think of it as Russian. Indeed, one cultivated variety of the domesticated sunflower is called 'Mammoth Russian', and most of the world's sunflowers for oil production are grown in Russia. It is also already the state flower of Kansas, but that shouldn't hinder its adoption as our national flower. However, the rose was selected, and although there are roses native to the United States, the one chosen is a cultivated rose from Europe. I still feel that a native

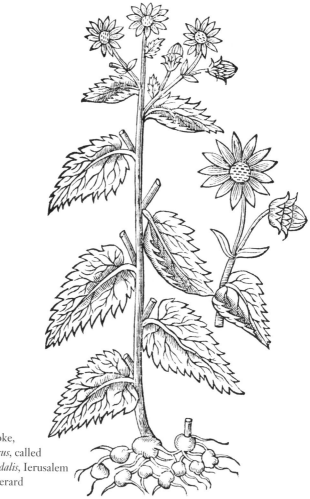

Jerusalem artichoke,
Helianthus tuberosus, called
"*Flos Solis Pyramidalis*, Ierusalem
Artichoke," by Gerard

plant is more worthy of the honor, although I must admit that many people in this country, like the rose, trace their ancestry to Europe.

The Jerusalem artichoke (*Helianthus tuberosus*) is another species of sunflower that is weedy in our area, but although I have grown it in my garden for more than forty years it has never become a weed there. In central Europe, however, it has become an invasive plant. In spite of its being a perennial, I have difficulty keeping the cultivated form growing more than a year, for field mice and voles find the tubers an attractive food. I once dug up a nest that contained more than thirty tubers. Like the common sunflower, it has also become a domesticated food plant, albeit a very minor one.

Confederate Daisy or Confederate Sunflower
Helianthus porteri

The Names. Confederate because it is native to areas that were in the Confederate States of America; daisy because it has daisy-like flower heads. The plant has been placed in three different genera (none of which has species called daisy). It was not recognized as belonging to *Helianthus* until fairly recently. The species epithet has been the same since 1849 when it was first described, named after Thomas Conrad Porter, who had collected it on Stone Mountain, Georgia. I am proposing a new common name, Confederate sunflower, because most species of *Helianthus* have sunflower as part of the common name. Or perhaps it would be even better to call it Porter's sunflower. Some people think it is time to forget the Confederacy. I am well aware that this plant will probably continue to be called by name Confederate daisy, however. There is also a Confederate rose. Does it belong to the genus *Rosa*? No, it is *Hibiscus mutabilis*, which is not even a native of the former Confederate States but of China!

The Time and Place. Early fall. Georgia, Alabama, and outlying stations in South Carolina.

The Description. Annual with many heads, ray and disk flowers yellow; leaves very narrow, nearly sessile. The one character that separates Confederate sunflower from all others is that the seed (achene, the fruit) has no awns (pappus) on its summit.

The Virtues. Confederate sunflower is very ornamental and flowers late in the season when few other plants are in bloom. In 1958, I brought it into cultivation in my garden from seeds from Georgia for I thought it was closely related to sunflowers, and in 1979 I decided that it belonged to the genus *Helianthus.* Although in nature this plant has a very restricted distribution on granite outcrops considerably to the south of Indiana, it has done well at Bloomington. Volunteers last only one or two years after it is grown, but in my home garden and that of my colleague, Carlos Miller, it has appeared for many years. We have both received compliments on its beauty from our neighbors. I can't resist quoting a remark of one of the reviewers of the manuscript: "Come now this is hardly a weed!"

Sumpweed or Marsh Elder *Iva annua*
PLATE 10

The Names. This plant usually grows in wet places, hence sump in the sense of a swamp, as well as marsh. The plant in no way I know of resembles our elder (elderberry, *Sambucus canadensis*) and for the present, elder as part of the name has to remain unexplained. There is also no satisfactory explanation of the name *Iva* insofar as I know. I have never met anyone who used either common name, and the plant is not well known among botanists, who, of course, usually use the scientific name.

The Time and Place. Late summer. Native to the east-central United States. Deam (1940) lists this plant only for Posey County in southern Indiana, but I found a large colony in Greene County, some twenty-five miles west of Bloomington in 1956 where it still exists. It has since been reported for three other counties (Yatskievych, 2000). I must, unfortunately, take blame for introducing the weed into the experimental field, for on several occasions I have deliberately grown it there for study. In spite of the fact that in nature it nearly always grows where there is considerable moisture, it does well in relatively dry places in the field and persists to this day. However, I am happy to report that it has not spread outside.

The Description. Annual, generally three to four feet tall; broad, mostly opposite, toothed leaves; heads greenish white, inconspicuous, and in dense spikes. Some people on first seeing sumpweed think it is some kind of ragweed, but our weedy ragweeds have lobed or deeply divided leaves and larger, tuberculate fruiting structures whereas sumpweed has smaller, nontuberculate seeds (fruits). Moreover, all the heads in the latter are alike, and in the ragweeds they are of two kinds (male and female).

The Virtues. Like ragweed, the pollen of sumpweed causes hay fever, so the virtues of this plant, if any, are few today. But in prehistoric times the seeds, which are rich in oil and protein, were an important source of food to the Indians of eastern North America. The oldest seeds in the archaeological record are the same size as those we find today, but as one comes up through time the size increases greatly, so it is concluded that sumpweed became a domesticated plant, deliberately cultivated and improved by the Indians. Little more than that can be said about the plants, for they, unlike most of the cultivated food crops of the Indians, were never observed by the Europeans. Apparently, the Indians had abandoned its cultivation, perhaps because other food plants, corn and beans, for example, that arrived from Mexico proved to be superior. One, I suppose, might also suggest that the Indians gave it up because they realized that it caused hay fever.

Although other species of marsh elder were used in Indian medicine, I can find no uses given for sumpweed. I would be surprised if it had not been used in some way. All parts of the plant have a strong camphor-like odor, and most strong-smelling plants found some use in medicine.

Prickly Lettuce *Lactuca serriola*

The Names. The English common name comes from the Old French *laitues,* which in turn stems from the ancient Latin name of the plant, *lactuca,* from *lac,* milk, because of the milky juice. Linnaeus originally spelled the specific epithet *serriola* and later correc_ed it to *scariola* (an old Arabian name). The latter spelling is still found in many books but his original spelling is the form that should be used.

The Time and Place. Late summer. From Europe. Prickly lettuce is a very common weed in my garden. According to Deam (1940) it appeared in Indiana in 1890 and in a few years had become an obnoxious weed throughout the state.

The Description. Annual, three or more feet high; stems spiny below; leaves unlobed to deeply divided, clasping the stem, midribs and margins spiny; heads small, all flowers ray-like, light yellow; seeds (fruits) beaked, with many slender hairs on the top that serve for wind dispersal; juice milky. In the sun, the leaves often twist so that they become perpendicular rather than parallel to the ground.

Prickly lettuce, *Lactuca serriola*, called "*Lactuca sylvestris foliis dissectis*, The wilde Lettuce with the diuided Leafe," by Gerard

The Virtues. The weed is very closely related to cultivated lettuce (*Lactuca sativa*), the world's most important salad plant, and the greatest virtue of prickly lettuce is that it likely participated directly, or indirectly through hybridization, in the origin of the cultivated plant. According to some friends of mine, the young leaves of prickly lettuce make a more tasty salad than the cultivated plant. It can also be used for honeymoon salad, that is, Lettuce [let us] alone without dressing. I have never had any desire to eat wild lettuce; I think it must be the spiny midribs that turn me off. The young stems and leaves can also be cooked as greens.

Wild lettuces had a number of uses in medicine. The early writers considered it narcotic and recommended it for sedation. The milky juice is slightly soporific. Gerard says, "Lettuce cooleth the heate of the stomacke, called the heart-burning; and helpeth it when it is troubled with choller; it quencheth thirst, causeth sleepe, maketh plenty of milke in nurses, ..." The Fox Indians gave it to women after childbirth to increase the flow of milk. The question one must ask: Did they discover this use independently or did they acquire it from the European settlers?

A European wild lettuce (*Lactuca virosa*, meaning, among other things, poisonous), sometimes cultivated for medicinal purposes, is poisonous. Fortunately, it is very rare in North America.

Pineapple Weed *Matricaria discoidea*

The Names. Pineapple comes from the odor. Deam (1940) gives the common name as rayless chamomile. When it is not in flower, it looks rather like chamomile (*Anthemis cotula*), the odor of which is decidedly unpleasant. *Matricaria* is from the Greek *matrix*, womb, from the reputed medicinal property of another species; *discoidea* is because all of the flowers are discoid, or tubular. When I learned this plant its name was *Matricaria matricarioides*. I rather liked the sound of it, although it was somewhat redundant. Why did the name change? I'll save the explanation for another book—a very boring one.

The Time and Place. Early summer. Native to the Pacific Coast of North America.

The Description. Annual about three to ten inches tall; leaves much divided; small yellow conical heads without rays. The pineapple odor is also characteristic.

The Virtues. Pineapple weed was used in many Indian medicines, but its chief virtue as far as I am concerned is the delightful odor. To perceive it, crush a head or leaves between the fingers before smelling. For some reason I do this every year.

Butterweed *Packera glabella*

The Names. Butterweed and yellowtop, which it is also sometimes called, are descriptive of the flower heads. *Packera* is named for John G. Packer, contemporary Canadian botanist; *glabella* means almost smooth, referring to the lack of hairs. All members of the genus are sometimes called ragwort, rag referring to the ragged appearance of the leaves, and wort, Anglo-Saxon for plant or herb or groundsel (from the Old English *grundesweilge*, meaning "ground swell over," referring to the way it spreads to take over the ground). Until very recently this plant was known as *Senecio glabellus*.

The Time and Place. Spring. Native to the central and southeastern United States. Butterweed was rare in our part of Indiana until about 1985 and has since become abundant. I once saw a field in the country covered with yellow flowers, which at first I thought was a mustard. It invaded my garden about 1990 but has never appeared in any great numbers.

The Description. Annual, generally six inches to three and a half feet tall; stems usually single, hollow; leaves alternate, deeply divided, with mostly rounded lobes, becoming progressively smaller farther up the stem; ray and disk flowers yellow, rather showy.

The Virtues. Most of our ragworts are spring wildflowers, and a few of the species are grown as ornamentals. No medicinal uses among the Indians are reported for butterweed, but other species were so used. The common groundsel (*Senecio vulgaris*), native to Europe, had many medicinal uses there and it is now a common weed in many parts of the eastern United States. In the old days, fairies rode on a branch of ragwort in Ireland and Scotland.

Goldenrod *Solidago canadensis*

The Names. The meaning of the common name is fairly obvious —spikes of golden flower heads adorn the plant—and very apt. One Eurasian species is *Solidago virgaurea*, the specific epithet of which translates as goldenrod. *Solidago* comes from the Latin *solidus* and probably means "to make whole" in allusion to its supposed medicinal value. Some people call *S. canadensis* tall or Canadian goldenrod to distinguish it from the many other goldenrods.

The Time and Place. Late summer. Native to much of North America. This goldenrod is a recent entry to my garden and there are only a few plants.

The Description. Perennial, generally two to five feet tall, much branched; numerous small yellow heads with both ray and disk flowers.

The Virtues. Several species are grown occasionally as ornamentals, more so in Europe than the United States, for goldenrods are so common here that they are little appreciated. It is an attractive plant, not only in flower but even into December when it is in fruit. Some people avoid goldenrods because they mistakenly think they are responsible for hay fever. Goldenrods are pollinated by insects; wind-pollinated plants are usually the culprits for allergies. Several species, including *Solidago canadensis*, had use in Indian medicine. This species often occurs along roadsides and is hardly a serious weed where I know it, but it is listed as an invasive species in central Europe.

Sow Thistle *Sonchus oleraceus* and *S. asper*

The Names. Called thistle because of spiny margins of the leaves, and sow because it is eaten by pigs. *Sonchus* is the ancient Greek name. In my garden there are two species: common sow thistle (*Sonchus oleraceus*, "fit for a vegetable") and spiny-leaf or prickly sow thistle (*S. asper*, "rough," because of the rugose or rough leaves).

The Time and Place. Summer. Both from Europe.

The Description. Annuals, generally one to several feet tall, rather similar to the weedy lettuce (*Lactuca serrata*) but heads larger with more numerous flowers, and seeds (fruits) without beaks and more numerous soft hairs on top; milky juice present. The common sow thistle (*Sonchus oleraceus*) is less prickly than the prickly sow thistle (*S. asper*) and has tuberculate or rough-ened seeds whereas those of the latter are merely nerved or ribbed.

The Virtues. Like lettuce, the sow thistles were given to nursing mothers to increase their milk. Other plants with a milky juice,

Sow thistle, *Sonchus asper*, called "*Sonchus asper*, Prickly Sow-thistle," by Gerard

unless they were known to be poisonous, were once used for the same purpose, for the milk in the plant was taken as a sign from the Creator for its use. These plants had a few other medicinal uses in Europe, and the juice of the common sow thistle (*Sonchus oleraceus*) was used as a cosmetic. The Indians also found some medicinal uses for these species, but I do not find increasing the flow of milk in new mothers among them.

Both species can be used for salads or as potherbs, but the leaves are too bitter to make them desirable for such purposes. In addition to pigs, many other animals may eat the plants, and the plants are sometimes deliberately gathered to feed rabbits.

The common sow thistle (*Sonchus oleraceus*) is one of the world's worst weeds (Holm et al., 1977). A third species, *S. arvensis* ("of cultivated ground"), also from Europe and now a weed in much of North America, is a perennial and spreads from underground creeping rootstocks that make it more difficult to eradicate than the annual species.

Dandelion *Taraxacum officinale*

The Names. The common name is from the French, *dent de lion*, tooth of the lion, which according to most accounts refers to the teeth on the leaf. Another common English name, pissabed, is from a Dutch word and may be descriptive of the result of eating it, for among its many medicinal effects, one is as a diuretic. The authorities do not agree on the source of the name *Taraxacum;* one says from an Arabian name. *Officinale* means officinal, or used in medicine.

The Time and Place. Spring and summer. *Taraxacum officinale* comes from Europe; some species are native to North America.

Dwarf dandelions (various species of *Krigia*), however, belong to another genus.

The Description. Does this common lawn weed need a description? Perhaps some of the people from the inner city of New York or Chicago have never seen it. Dandelion is a perennial

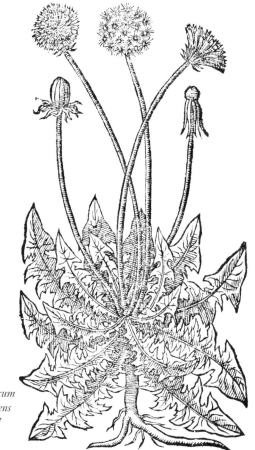

Dandelion, *Taraxacum officinale*, called "*Dens Leonis*, Dandelion," by Gerard

from a deep-seated taproot. The leaves are all basal and irregularly toothed. The yellow flower heads are borne on a hollow stalk, a few to several inches high. I have seen these stalks two feet long in old fields, and lengths exceeding that have been secured by altering the growing conditions in contests with prizes for the longest. The beak of the ripe seed has several very slender hairs that serve for wind dispersal. The plants contain a milky juice.

The Virtues. Few children have not puffed the seeds from the heads. The number of puffs required to remove them were once thought to indicate the hour of the day or the number of spouses one would have. The flower heads are beautiful, I think, and many people agree with me, but as cut flowers they are not very satisfactory for they wilt rapidly. When they go to seed, the plants are unattractive. Because most people favor a lawn that is a solid, even green, dandelions have become despised, perhaps more so than any other plant unless it be crabgrass (*Digitaria*). Mowing may cut off the seed heads, sometimes not on the first try, but it rarely touches the leaves, which are flat on the surface of the ground. Digging them out is not very effective, for unless one gets the entire root the part left will regenerate a new plant. Weed killers are the only easy and effective means of eliminating them. The plants, of course, reproduce readily by the wind-blown seeds, and most dandelions can produce seeds without pollination. In fact, the flower parts of the head can be cut off in an early stage and the seeds still mature. (I can't imagine why anyone would want to do this.)

There are few weeds that have had more uses for both food and medicine than dandelions. The very young leaves are widely employed as potherbs and may be grown intentionally for this purpose. It is probably best to rinse the leaves with boiling water to remove any bitterness before cooking. The leaves may be used as a salad, but better for this purpose are the young crowns of the plants with the green leaves removed. I find them delicious either raw or cooked in various ways. It is a time-consuming task to gather them, however, and I estimate that one would spend more calories gathering than one would derive from eating them. The roots can be cooked and are said to taste like parsnips (which doesn't recommend them to me). Also, dried and ground, the roots are said to make a very good substitute for coffee. The flower heads are used to make dandelion wine. I have sampled it only once so perhaps I shouldn't give an opinion, but I found it strong stuff, not from the alcoholic content but from the taste of dandelions. Another use for the flower heads, I learned from a colleague, is to dip them in batter and fry them.

The use of dandelion in medicine goes back to ancient times when it was used for many ailments. The Indians also have many such uses for it. Among other uses, Gerard tells us,

> Boiled, it strengthens the weake stomacke, and eaten raw it stops the bellie, and helpes the Dysentery, especially being boyled with Lentiles; The juice drunke is good against the vnuoluntary effusion of seed; boyled in vineger, it is good against the paine that troubles some in making of water; . . . .

Tons of the root are still imported to the United States for use in diet and digestive drinks and other tonics. Another, closely related species, *Taraxacum kok-saghyz*, has been grown as a rubber plant for its latex in Russia.

Ironweed *Vernonia gigantea*

PLATE I I

The Names. The iron part of the name is said to be from the very hard or tough stems. *Vernonia* is named for William Vernon, an English botanist who collected plants in Maryland in the seventeenth century; *gigantea*, of course, means gigantic. The plant is often called tall ironweed and the name once used, *V. altissima*, means very tall ironweed.

The Time and Place. Late summer and early fall. Native to the eastern United States. There are only a few ironweed plants in my garden in somewhat shady areas and only recently arrived.

The Description. Perennial, generally four to six feet tall; stem often red or purple; leaves alternate, lance-shaped with no or very short stalks; heads many with purple tubular flowers.

The Virtues. In flower, ironweed is a rather attractive plant. I find no uses reported for it in Indian medicine, although other species of the genus were so used.

Cocklebur or Clotbur *Xanthium strumarium*

PLATE I 2

The Names. I have not been able to trace when the name cocklebur was first used for this plant. Gerard placed it in the same "genus" as burdock (*Arctium minus*) and called it the "lesser Burre Docke." Cockle is the name used for any weed in corn. (Corn is the name for the common cereal in English; in Great Britain it is used for wheat, except in Scotland where it refers to oats.) In some places in England both cocklebur and clotbur are used for agrimony (*Agrimonia eupatoria*), which belongs to the rose family. *Xanthium* comes from the Greek *xanthos*, yellow, and xanthium was the name of a plant used to dye the hair; *strumarium* is because this plant was supposed to cure *strumae*, tumors. Other specific epithets are often used for this plant in weed books.

The Time and Place. Flowering in late summer and fruiting in the fall. Native to much of North America. It was introduced into Europe and is weedy, although one race of it may be native there. I know exactly how the cocklebur got into the garden. I had never seen it before 1960, although it occurs around Bloomington, usually in low, wet places. Then at that time, Carlos Miller, our plant physiologist, decided that he should renew his supply of cockleburs. This plant has been very important in research, particularly in the study of the flowering process. Since the year in which he planted them, we have had anywhere from a dozen to fifty plants come up spontaneously. They are usually mostly eliminated by hoeing or mowing but the plants still come up from old seeds buried in the soil even if the new crop of weeds do not produce mature seeds in some years.

The Description. Annual, usually only a foot or two high but reaching six feet at times; leaves alternate, rather broad and sometimes lobed; flower heads either male or female and borne on the same plant. The very small male heads resemble those of ragweed (*Ambrosia*); the female heads form globular burs, one-half to nearly an inch long; the body of the bur varies from densely hairy to nearly hairless and has many hooked prickles. The cocklebur, like other wind-pollinated members of the aster family, looks quite unlike other members of the family that are adapted for insect pollination.

The burs contain two seeds; one will germinate the following year and the second remains dormant until the second or subsequent years. In addition to a very efficient method of seed dispersal by animals, the burs will also float, so water dispersal may occur.

The Virtues. The plant was used in Indian medicine. Eating the leaves has been suspected of causing poisoning in livestock. Cer-

Cocklebur, *Xanthium strumarium*, called "*Bardana minor,* The lesse Burre Docke," by Gerard

tainly one of the great virtues of cocklebur is that it led to the invention of Velcro, the best fastener since the zipper. In the 1940s, George de Mestral, a Swiss engineer, after a walk found cockleburs on his trousers and his dog. He decided to examine them under magnification and found that they were covered with tiny hooks. He then figured out how to weave nylon so that the hooks on one side engaged loops on the other. Thus was born Velcro (from the French *velours* and *crochet*, meaning hooked velvet).

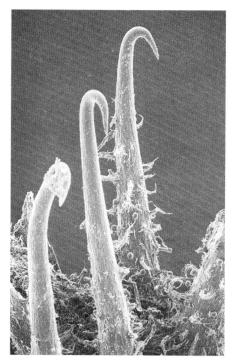

Prickles on the bur of cocklebur (*Xanthium strumarium*), ×28, scanning electron micrograph by W. Rudolf Turner

PLATE 1. Pigweed, *Amaranthus hybridus* (Amaranthaceae), a hybrid of the weedy smooth pigweed and a red ornamental form

PLATE 2. Poison ivy, *Toxicodendron radicans* (Anacardiaceae)

PLATE 3. Goutweed, *Aegopodium podagraria* (Apiaceae)

PLATE 4. Queen Anne's lace, *Daucus carota* (Apiaceae)

PLATE 5. Pipevine, *Aristolochia tomentosa* (Aristolochiaceae)

PLATE 6. Milkweed, *Asclepias syriaca* (Asclepiadaceae)

PLATE 7. Daisy, *Chrysanthemum leucanthemum* (Asteraceae)

PLATE 8. Thistle, *Cirsium vulgare* (Asteraceae)

PLATE 9. Sunflower, *Helianthus annuus* (Asteraceae), with American goldfinch

PLATE 10. Sumpweed, *Iva annua* (Asteraceae)

PLATE 11. Ironweed, *Vernonia gigantea* (Asteraceae)

PLATE 13. Japanese honeysuckle, *Lonicera japonica* (Caprifoliaceae)

PLATE 12. Cocklebur, *Xanthium strumarium* (Asteraceae)

PLATE 14. Bush honeysuckle, *Lonicera maackii* (Caprifoliaceae)

PLATE 15. Elderberry, *Sambucus canadensis* (Caprifoliaceae)

PLATE 16. Field bindweed, *Convolvulus arvensis* (Convolvulaceae)

PLATE 17. Sassafras, *Sassafras albidum* (Lauraceae); note the three leaf shapes

PLATE 18. Orange daylily,
Hemerocallis fulva (Liliaceae)

PLATE 19. Star-of-Bethlehem,
Ornithogalum umbellatum (Liliaceae)

PLATE 20. Devil's claw, *Proboscidea parviflora* (Pedaliaceae)

PLATE 21. Pokeweed, *Phytolacca americana* (Phytolaccaceae)

PLATE 22. Green foxtail, *Setaria viridis* (Poaceae)

PLATE 23. Spring beauty, *Claytonia virginica* (Portulacaceae)

PLATE 24. Black cherry, *Prunus serotina* (Rosaceae)

PLATE 25. Jimsonweed, *Datura stramonium* (Solanaceae), in flower with hawkmoth

PLATE 26. Thorn apple, *Datura stramonium* (Solanaceae), in fruit

PLATE 27. Horse nettle, *Solanum carolinense* (Solanaceae), in flower

PLATE 28. Horse nettle, *Solanum carolinense* (Solanaceae), in fruit

PLATE 29. Virginia creeper, *Parthenocissus quinquefolia* (Vitaceae), in fall

Brassicaceae Mustard Family

Mostly herbs with alternate leaves; flowers several to many, usually with four separate petals, frequently in the form of a cross or crucifer (hence the family's older name, Cruciferae); six stamens of two lengths; fruit narrow, elongate or round, pod-like, dry at maturity and containing few to many seeds. The Brassicaceae include a large number of food plants and ornamentals as well as weeds. Among the better known foods are the mustards (also a condiment), cabbage, cauliflower, broccoli, Brussels sprouts, turnip, radish, and watercress. To this family also belongs a most important organism for research, *Arabidopsis thaliana*, mouse-ear cress, native to Europe and used to study genetics and development. Although this plant is a weed in much of North America, it is not in my garden. It is grown, however, in many laboratories in Jordan Hall, the building that houses the Department of Biology at Indiana University.

Winter Cress or Yellow Rocket *Barbarea vulgaris*

The Names. The common or bitter winter cress is one of many cresses. Cress is from an Old English word meaning to nibble or to eat. Rocket apparently was first used for another genus in the mustard family, *Eruca*, and the word was taken from the French *roquette*. Our plant has also been called spring mustard, mustard coming from the French *moutarde*. *Barbarea* is from St. Barbara, a virgin martyr of the early Christian church.

The Time and Place. Spring. From Eurasia. Winter cress has been a very common weed in my garden since the early years.

The Description. In books it is said to be a biennial or short-lived perennial but I think it is often an annual in my garden, where it is usually two to three feet tall; leaves divided into rounded lobes with the terminal one the largest, base of the leaf clasping the stem and going part way around it; flowers bright yellow; pods slender, about an inch long.

The Virtues. The plant was once called herb of St. Barbara, perhaps because the plant was green and could be eaten on the day of her festival, December 4 (Grigson, 1955), or because the seeds of a related species were planted on that day in western Europe (Fernald, 1950). Winter cress can be eaten when young as a potherb, best boiled in two changes of water to remove the bitterness. Also, it can be used as a salad plant if one can tolerate the bitterness. When I first returned to Indiana after two years in California I thought that this plant was some kind of mustard (*Brassica*) and I found that many people called it wild mustard. Sometimes whole fields are colored yellow with it.

Shepherd's Purse *Capsella bursa-pastoris*

The Names. Shepherd's purse is so called because the pod is shaped like a shepherd's purse. Would that all common names were so logical! I hope this explanation is correct; I have never seen a shepherd's purse and, for that matter, very few shepherds. *Capsella* is from *capsa*, Latin for box; *bursa-pastoris* means "pouch of the shepherd."

The Time and Place. Spring. From Europe.

The Description. Annual; leaves forming a rosette, stem leaves smaller, variable in shape, often toothed or even deeply cleft, lobed at the base and clasping the stem; petals small, white; pod triangular or heart-shaped.

The Virtues. The young foliage or the whole plant may be used for greens. Shepherd's purse had many medicinal uses in Europe. From Gerard we learn that

> Shepheards purse stayeth bleeding in any part of the body; . . . it healeth greene and bleeding wounds: it is

Shepherd's purse,
Capsella bursa-pastoris,
called "*Bursa Pastoris,*
Shepheards purse,"
by Gerard

maruellous good for inflammations new begun, and for all diseases which must be checked backe and cooled . . . [It] doth stop the laske, the spitting and pissing of bloud, and all other fluxes of bloud.

Later in America the Indians also found medicinal uses for it. If one picks one of the little heart-shaped pods, a mature one, it breaks and the seeds scatter out. This feature has led to the names mother's heart and pick-your-mother's-heart-out in England. Children would play a "cruel little game" in which one child told another to pick one of the pods, which, of course, would break, and then he would be told that he had broken his mother's heart. For more information on these and other names of this plant—naughty men's plaything is my favorite—see Grigson's (1955) *The Englishman's Flora.* Shepherd's purse is one of the world's worst weeds (Holm et al., 1977).

Whitlow Grass *Draba verna*

The Names. The common name comes from its use for treating whitlows. *Draba* is from *drabe*, acrid, an old Greek name used for some cress; *verna* means "of the spring" and is very fitting.

The Time and Place. March and April. From Eurasia.

The Description. Tiny plants with all the leaves at the base; flowering stalks only an inch to a few inches high; petals white, parted nearly to the middle; pods nearly flat, slightly longer than broad.

The Virtues. The only thing that Gerard could say for this plant was that it was used "to heale the disease of the nailes called Whitlow." A whitlow is an inflammation of the fingers or toes, in some forms affecting the nails of humans or hooves of domestic animals. The origin of the word whitlow remains unexplained. In my garden, this little weed usually occurs in the poorer soil, where I welcome it every year as a sign of spring. Several other species of *Draba* are cultivated, most often for rock or alpine gardens.

Peppergrass or Pepperweed *Lepidium campestre*

The Names. The seeds have a peppery taste. Many plants that are not members of the grass family are called grass. Frequently, they have grass-like leaves. This one does not, however, so the name pepperweed is to be preferred. *Lepidium* is from the Greek *lepidion*, small scale, referring to the scale-like pods; *campestre* means "of the fields."

The Time and Place. Late spring and early summer. From Europe.

The Description. Annual, one to two feet tall, most parts densely short hairy; leaves somewhat lance-shaped, those of the stem clasping the stem and lobed at the base; petals small, white; small pod slightly longer than broad with a slight rim on the top.

The Virtues. Young shoots of pepperweed have been used as a substitute for watercress (*Nasturtium officinale*). The seeds, mixed with vinegar and salt, are said to make a tasty dressing for meat. Poor man's pepper (*Lepidium virginicum*), native to much of North America, is also a weed in the area of Bloomington and may have occurred in the experimental field in the past. It is most readily distinguished from pepperweed by having non-clasping stem leaves. The pods of pepperweed become horizontal at maturity, and raindrops hitting them cause the seeds to shoot out of the pod.

Virginia Rock Cress *Sibara virginica*

The Names. Although Deam (1940) uses the name Virginia rock cress, neither Fernald (1950) nor Gleason and Cronquist (1991) give a common name. As we have seen under winter cress (*Barbarea vulgaris*), cress means to nibble or eat. I don't know that this cress is nibbled or eaten but it is called that because the name cress is used for species of the genus *Arabis*. Our plant was at one time placed in *Arabis* but now it is recognized as sufficiently different to belong to another genus, whose name was formed by spelling *Arabis* backward. Such names are entirely legal, for according to the *International Code of Botanical Nomenclature*, the name of a genus "may be taken from any source whatever, and may even be composed in an absolutely arbitrary manner." The author of the name *Sibara* was E. L. Greene, who explained that it is an anagram, but more than that it is an ananym.

The Time and Place. Early spring. Native to the central and southern United States.

The Description. Annual or biennial, four to six inches tall, unbranched or branching from base; leaves mostly at the base, deeply divided into five or seven parts; petals white to purple; stamens four; pods slender, stiff, one-half to an inch long, purple when young; seeds explosively dispersed.

The Virtues. I had not seen this plant until 1992 in which year it appeared in some abundance in both the garden and my yard at home. Deam (1940) does not give it for Monroe County, where

Indiana University is, but the plant was collected on campus in 1984 by a student, David Darrow. I am rather sorry that I ever found it for I am unable to report any virtues, although I can say that as yet it does not appear to be a serious weed.

Campanulaceae Bellflower Family

Mostly herbs with five petals, united at least at the base, all alike or some differing in size or shape; ovary beneath the other flower parts; fruit a capsule with many seeds; sometimes a milky juice present. Several members of the family are cultivated for their delightful flowers, the best known being the bellflower (*Campanula*) and the lobelias (*Lobelia*).

Indian Tobacco *Lobelia inflata*

The Names. The common name comes from the smoking of the leaves by Indians for the narcotic effect or from the tobacco-like sensation when the leaves are chewed. *Lobelia* is in honor of the herbalist Matthias de L'Obel (1538–1616), whose name in Latin is Lobelius; *inflata* is because of the swollen or inflated fruit, a capsule.

The Time and Place. Summer. Native to eastern North America.

The Description. Annual, six inches to two feet tall, hairy; leaves longer than broad, toothed, unstalked or short-stalked; corolla blue or white, two-lipped; capsule nearly globular, opening at or near the top.

The Virtues. This plant was much used medicinally. Indians smoked it or used an infusion of it to break the tobacco or whiskey habit, and among the Iroquois it was used both as a love and antilove potion. It was also used in medicine in England after its introduction there in 1829. Indian tobacco was particularly popular for the treatment of asthma and is sometimes called asthma weed. A tea that is both a "relaxant and a stimulant" was made from it, according to Duke (1985). The plants contain a number of alkaloids, and one of these, lobeline, is used today in preparations for breaking nicotine dependence. Overdoses of the plant are toxic, and death could result.

Venus's Looking Glass *Triodanis perfoliata*

The Names. Some books give no common name for *Triodanis perfoliata*. I learned it as Venus's looking glass and decided that it was so called because the little flower was Venus and the facing leaf was the mirror. I have found no support for such a notion and I now think the name has been transferred to it from the European species, *Legousia* or *Specularia*. Both species at one time were placed in the genus *Specularia*. Why is the Old World species called Venus's looking glass? Grigson gives the name Venus's looking glass for *L. hybrida*, in 1955 indicating that the polished, oval seed resembles a speculum but in 1974 writing that the name is descriptive of the flower's topping its long ovary. So take your choice. *Triodanis* means having three unequal teeth, descriptive of the calyx of some species; *perfoliata* refers to the stem's apparently passing through the leaves.

The Time and Place. Late spring and early summer. Native to much of North America but perhaps originally from tropical America.

The Description. Annual, a few inches to one and a half feet tall, somewhat hairy; flowers in the axils of leaves, lobes of the corolla spreading, purple or lavender; leaves clasping the stem, about as broad as long.

The Virtues. This to me rather attractive little weed was used for dyspepsia by the Cherokee and as an emetic by the Fox.

European Venus's looking glass, *Specularia speculum-veneris*, called "*Speculum Veneris*, Venus Looking-glasse," by Gerard

Caprifolicaceae Honeysuckle Family

Mostly shrubs or woody vines with opposite leaves without stipules; flowers tubular, usually five-lobed, symmetrical or asymmetrical, the ovary partially or entirely below the level of the other flower parts. The honeysuckle family includes a number of plants grown for ornament, including species of elder (*Sambucus*), twinflower (*Linnaea*), snowberry (*Symphoricarpos*), and *Viburnum*.

Japanese Honeysuckle *Lonicera japonica*

PLATE 13

The Names. Honeysuckle is the name originally given to an English species whose nectar, the honey, was sucked from the corolla tube. The genus name honors Adam Lonitzer, a German physician and naturalist of the sixteenth century.

The Time and Place. Late spring and early summer but may continue to produce a few flowers into fall. Native to Asia.

The Description. Climbing or trailing vine, hairy; leaves short-stalked, oval or oblong; corolla white, sometimes with purple tinge, becoming yellow or cream; berries black.

The Virtues. Some people think the fragrance of honeysuckle is unequaled, and it was planted for this reason as well as for the attractive flowers. Unfortunately, it has escaped to become, as Fernald (1950) says, "a most pernicious and dangerous weed, overwhelming and strangling the native flora and most difficult to eradicate; extensively planted and encouraged by those who do not value the rapidly destroyed indigenous vegetation." Today it is included with the invasive species. It came to the experimental field uninvited and also to my home garden where I tried to eliminate it without success. It reproduces by seed as well as spreading extensively by vegetative means. The plant was used for medicine in Asia.

Just outside the fence at the field are some Amur honeysuckles or bush honeysuckles, as they are called in Indiana (although the latter name is perhaps better reserved for the genus *Diervilla*). Unlike Japanese honeysuckle, this species, *Lonicera maackii* (plate 14), is a bush, not a vine, and along with a couple of closely related species is now included with the worst invasive species found in Indiana and much of eastern North America. Originally, this species was introduced from Asia for its ornamental value; the paired red berries are very attractive. I expect it will be in the field before this book is published.

Elder or Elderberry *Sambucus canadensis*
PLATE 15

The Names. The word elder comes from England where it was used for a species native there (*Sambucus nigra*); the word is from the Old English *ellaern*. *Sambucus* is an old Latin name for the plant, perhaps from *sambuce*, a flute-like musical instrument that could be made from the stems.

The Time and Place. June and July. Native to much of North America. Our elder was introduced into England in 1761.

The Description. Shrub only slightly woody, five to ten feet tall; leaves of five to eleven pointed, toothed, lance-shaped leaflets; large, flat-topped flower clusters; flowers many, corolla white, small, fragrant; fruits rather small, berry-like, purple-black.

The Virtues. Nearly all parts of elder were used medicinally by the Indians for a great variety of complaints. It was adopted as a medicinal plant by the European settlers, and Millspaugh (1892) says that in domestic medicine it became almost a pharmacy in itself. The fruits are used for the juice, to make wine (it was elderberry wine that was spiked with poison in *Arsenic and Old Lace*), and for jellies and pies. For pies it is said that elderberries are best if the fruits are allowed to dry before using. The flowers have been added to pancakes. Some caution should be used, however, for all parts of the plant, including the unripe fruits, contain a poisonous alkaloid and a cyanogenic glucoside. Children have been poisoned by using blowguns and whistles made from the stems, according to Hardin and Arena (1969). *Sambucus canadensis* and several other species are occasionally cultivated as ornamentals.

As interesting as our plant is, it is far less so than the English black elder, which has much mythology, folklore, magic and superstition associated with it. Grieve (1959) devotes more than ten pages to it in her *Modern Herbal.*

Caryophyllaceae Pink Family

Mostly herbs; leaves opposite, untoothed; stems often slightly swollen at the point of leaf attachment; petals usually present, separate, four or five, but sometimes so deeply lobed as to appear twice as many; fruit a small capsule, splitting along three or more lines with many small seeds usually attached to a central stalk. The pink family furnishes us a number of ornamentals such as carnation (*Dianthus caryophyllus*), sweet William (*D. barbatus*), several kinds of pinks (other species of *Dianthus*), and baby's breath (*Gypsophila paniculata*).

Bouncing Bet or Soapwort *Saponaria officinalis*

The Names. Who inspired the name bouncing Bett (as it is written in England) remains unknown, but I learn from Mrs. William Starr Dana (1893) that the feminine comeliness and bounce of the plant suggest a Yorkshire housemaid. The name soapwort is readily explained for the plant forms a lather with water and has been used as a soap. *Saponaria* has the same origin, for *sapo* means soap in Latin; *officinalis* is translated as "of the shops" by Fernald (1950), and Bailey (1949) gives "officinal, medicinal." Many plants bearing this specific epithet were apparently sold in shops for medicinal use.

The Time and Place. Early to midsummer. From Europe, originally introduced into North America as a cultivated plant. It no longer grows in my garden but is still common near there.

The Description. Perennial, forming colonies from the rootstocks, two to three feet tall; leaves oval- to lance-shaped; flowers several, showy; petals five, pink to white, fragrant (doubled forms are known).

The Virtues. This rather attractive weed is still sometimes "planted in gardens for the floures sake," as Gerard says of "sopewort." Its chief use has been as a soap; its mucilaginous juice contains saponins, which are responsible for the suds when mixed with water. It was also used as a medicine both by Europeans and the Indians. Gerard tells us that a decoction of it was used against the French pox, an Old English name for syphilis.

Chickweed *Stellaria media*

The Names. Chickweed because it is eaten by chickens. Other birds are also fond of the seeds. *Stellaria* is from *stella*, star, in reference to the star-like flower shape; *media* means intermediate.

Chickweed,
Stellaria media,
called "*Alsine maior*,
Great Chickweed,"
by Gerard

The Time and Place. Very early to late spring and sometimes in fall and winter. We have a colony of plants next to the greenhouse at the experimental field that I have found in bloom in January in some years. From Eurasia.

The Description. Small, matted annual or short-lived perennial with nearly oval leaves; flowers few, with white petals and three styles; capsule short, round, opening by six valves.

The Virtues. Young stems and leaves may be cooked as a potherb or used raw in salads. This is a valuable medicinal plant according to the herbalists. Preparations labeled chickweed are found in local stores. Two uses for it are mentioned in Indian medicine. Another introduced species, *Stellaria holostea*, is sometimes grown for flower borders or as a ground cover under the name Easter bells. The common chickweed is one of the world's worst weeds (Holm et al., 1977) and it has practically a worldwide distribution today. It is not a bad weed in my garden, however. Although it is common there, it has a shallow root system and is easily eliminated by pulling it by hand or with the hoe when necessary.

Although I don't recall seeing the mouse-eared chickweed in my garden, it is to be expected there for it is a common weed in our area. It is sometimes confused with the common chickweed but is a slightly taller, more hairy plant with narrower leaves, flowers with five styles, and a longer, often curved capsule, opening at the top by ten teeth. I don't know why it is called mouse-eared (perhaps from the shape of the little leaves on the flowering stalks). Scientifically it is known as *Cerastium* (from the Greek *cerastes*, horned, in reference to the capsule) *fontanum* (of the spring or fountain). It comes to us from Europe.

Celastraceae Staff Tree Family

Woody plants, shrubs or climbers; leaves simple; flowers usually small, not showy; seeds usually covered with an aril (a fleshy or pulpy outgrowth). The American bittersweet (*Celastrus scandens*) belongs here. Several species of *Euonymus* (spindle tree) are cultivated. The oriental bittersweet (*C. orbiculatus*) is listed among the invasive species of Indiana (Anonymous, 2000); fortunately, it has not yet reached my garden.

Wintercreeper *Euonymus fortunei*

The Names. My standard reference (Fernald, 1950) fails to provide a common name, but wintercreeper is fairly widely used and not inappropriate for the plant creeps over the ground and is often green all winter. One horticulture book gives the name climbing euonymus, which is also satisfactory for the plant climbs trees as well as creeps. *Euonymus* is from the ancient Greek, meaning "good name," but Fernald tells us that the name was "used ironically, the plants having had the bad reputation of poisoning cattle"; *fortunei* is from Robert Fortune, British gardener of the nineteenth century who discovered this plant in China. He wrote several books about his collecting expeditions.

The Time and Place. Summer. From China.

The Description. Plants trailing over the ground or climbing by means of aerial roots; leaves opposite, more or less evergreen, leathery, elliptic, one to two inches long; flowers small, bisexual; sepals and petals four or five, greenish or purplish; capsule white (in my garden); seeds with scarlet covering (some people confuse the fruit and seeds with those of bittersweet, *Celastrus scandens*).

The Virtues. Wintercreeper is widely cultivated and comes in several horticultural varieties. It does make an excellent ground cover, growing over and usually crowding out all other vegetation. If people plan to try it, I would recommend that they have at least five feet of concrete on all sides of their plot. From a specimen in the herbarium I know that Charles Deam grew this in his garden at Bluffton, Indiana, in 1938, but it is not mentioned in his *Flora;* perhaps he had a well-behaved variety. How this species became established and a very serious weed in both the experimental field and my backyard at home, I do not know. At home I let it climb up my black cherry tree—I rather enjoyed seeing the fruit—but once the woody stems reached five inches in diameter I began to fear for the tree. Sawing through these stems wasn't easy. My wife resolved to eliminate it from the yard but it grew faster than she could remove it. We finally sold our house, but I am sorry to report that as I write this from our retirement cottage, I can look out my window and see it growing up a maple. I was not surprised to find that it is now listed as an invasive species in Indiana (Anonymous, 2000).

Chenopodiaceae Goosefoot Family

Mostly herbs; leaves alternate, often slightly fleshy; flowers very small, densely clustered, often greenish, lacking petals. The goosefoot family includes three important food plants: table and sugar beets (*Beta vulgaris*), spinach (*Spinacia oleracea*), and quinua (*Chenopodium quinoa*).

Wormseed or Mexican Tea *Chenopodium ambrosioides*

The Names. The seeds of this plant were, and probably still are, used as a vermifuge. In Mexico a tea is made from the leaves. For *Chenopodium* see the next entry on goosefoot; *ambrosioides* because of its resemblance (very slight) to *Ambrosia*, the ragweed.

The Time and Place. Summer. From Latin America.

The Description. Annual or short-lived perennial, one to three feet tall; leaves with yellow glands, giving the plant a very strong, pungent (and unpleasant to me) odor; seeds shiny brown.

The Virtues. Wormseed was a very important medicinal plant, used in many ways, particularly for intestinal worms, for which it was the usual treatment until the twentieth century. The plant was employed in many parts of the Americas as a vermifuge and was introduced into England for this purpose in 1732. All parts of the plant can be used, but the seeds are most effective. An overdose can be toxic, and too much can cause death—a warning to those who would attempt to use it. In addition to being used to make a tea in Mexico for soothing the nerves, it is also a favorite herb for flavoring a great variety of dishes. The plant is also still a favorite medicinal plant in many parts of Latin America. *Chenopodium ambrosioides* is an extremely variable species and many races have been recognized, some of which may well be good species. I have grown several collections from Mexico, where it is known as *epazote*, as well as from Ecuador, where it is called *paico*. The plants from the two countries are not only very different from each other but from the North American plant as well. I am not responsible for its being a weed in the experimental field for it grew there before I brought in plants from Latin America.

Goosefoot or Pigweed *Chenopodium berlandieri* and *C. missouriense*

The Names. Goosefoot because some species, but not these, have leaves the shape of a goose's foot; pigweed because pigs eat it. I would prefer to use the latter name for the amaranths, but there is nothing I can do to so limit it. Also, I prefer using chenopod as the common name rather than goosefoot. Some people also call these species lamb's-quarter, but that name originally belonged to another species, *Chenopodium album. Chenopodium* is Greek for goose's foot; *berlandieri* honors Jean Louis Berlandier, a French botanist of the nineteenth century who explored in Mexico and the Southwest.

The Time and Place. Late summer. Native to most of North America. *Chenopodium missouriense* has been in my garden since it was first established, but *C. berlandieri* did not occur there until 1973 when Hugh Wilson introduced it for his doctoral study. It has been with us every year since. *Chenopodium berlandieri* also occurs naturally in Indiana and is in Deam (1950) as *C. bushianum.*

The Description. Annuals, two to six feet tall; leaves oval or lance-shaped, relatively broad, somewhat white-mealy on the surface and generally with a few teeth; seeds roundish, shiny black. The species of goosefoot are rather difficult to tell apart. It is often necessary to examine the seed surface microscopically to make an identification. *Chenopodium missouriense* is generally the taller of the two, with slightly narrower, darker green leaves with little or no white-mealiness, and smaller seeds. In my garden, *C. berlandieri* suffers from a disease—viral, I suspect—that causes a distortion of the leaves.

The Virtues. Berlandier's chenopod was an important food plant of the Indians of the eastern United States for its seeds. It has been shown by archaeologists that in prehistoric time, Indians domesticated the wild plant and cultivated it extensively. However, it apparently disappeared as a cultivated plant about the time of the arrival of Europeans. Various races of it are still cultivated in Mexico. The seeds of the weedy species may be eaten whole or ground. A single plant produces a huge number of seeds and these may be collected readily, but then winnowing is required to remove the chaff, which can be very time-consuming. The seeds of chenopods contain saponins, bitter substances that give an undesirable taste. In South America the seeds of quinua are washed before cooking. My experiments have shown that Berlandier's chenopod contains less saponins than the Missouri chenopod.

A much better way of eating the weeds is as greens or potherbs. Many people have compared them to spinach, which, of course, belongs to the same family, but I think they are better than spinach. It is one of the few weeds that I would be willing to eat on a regular basis as a vegetable. One should be sure, however, to use only very young plants gathered in late spring or early summer. Many of the older books, and some of the more recent ones as well, list only lamb's-quarter (*Chenopodium album*) as a weed. That species, which is native to Europe, is one of the world's worst weeds (Holm et al., 1977). Lamb's-quarter also makes excellent greens, and at one time the seeds were eaten in Europe. From the analysis of the stomach contents of the Tollund man of the first century A.D. we know that the seeds formed part of his last meal before he ended up in a bog. His well-preserved body was found in a bog in Denmark, and he is thought to have died there from hanging. For people who would like to know more about the chenopods, see Heiser (1985).

Clusiaceae Mangosteen Family

Herbs, shrubs, and trees; leaves usually opposite, simple; flowers with four or five separate petals; stamens many; fruit a berry, drupe, or many-seeded capsule. A number of species of St.-John's-wort (*Hypericum*) are grown for their flowers. The mangosteen (*Garcina mangostana*) and the mamey (*Mammea americana*) are tropical trees grown for their fruits. When I learned my plant families, St.-John's-wort was placed in the Hypericaceae, or Guttiferae: now that family is considered merely a subfamily of Clusiaceae.

St.-John's-Wort or Klamath Weed *Hypericum perforatum*

The Names. The common name commemorates St. John because the plant blooms on or near St. John's Day, June 24. From my botanical sources I learn little of the origin of the name *Hypericum*. Bailey (1949) merely says that it is a Greek name of obscure origin. Grieve (1959) however, says the name means "over an apparition," for a whiff of it would cause an evil spirit to flee. *Perforatum* means perforated, from the glandular dots on the leaves.

The Time and Place. Summer. From Europe.

The Description. Perennial herb one to two feet tall; leaves about an inch long, narrow, without stalks; flowers numerous, yellow; fruit a capsule. The most distinctive feature is the presence of transparent or clear glands on the leaves. (I learned to describe these as "pellucid punctate" leaves in college, a phrase that sticks with me in spite of very infrequent usage.) These may be seen as dots if the leaves are held up to the light. They contain oil that gives the plant its distinctive odor. The petals of the common St.-John's-wort may also have black dots on their margins.

The Virtues. The plant is said to be one of the chief herbs of St. John the Baptist; it is one of the most famous of European plants, with many superstitions having grown up around it. Gathered on the eve of St. John's Day, it was hung on doors and in windows to protect the people from witchcraft—from all evils, in fact, including demon lovers—and it was considered an effective remedy for dispelling melancholy. St.-John's-wort also had much use in medicine. Gerard found it good for, among other things, burnings, scaldings, all wounds, and for "rotten and filthy" ulcers. There was, in fact, no better natural balsam for curing wounds, so he tells us, than the one that he made, and he proceeds to give his recipe:

> Take white wine two pintes, oyle oliue foure pounds, oile of Turpentine two pounds, the leaues, floures, and seeds of S. Iohns wort, of each two great handfulls gently bruised; put them all together into a great double glasse, and set it in the Sunne eight or ten dayes; then boyle them in the same glasse *per balneum Mariae*, that is, in a kettle of water with some straw in the bottome, wherein the glasse must stand to boyle: which done, straine the liquor from the herbes, and do as you did before, putting in the like quantitie of herbes, floures, and seeds, but not any more wine.

Fortunately, one doesn't have to go to such lengths to prepare it today. The corner drugstore will have an abundant supply already prepared, for it is now one of the most popular of the herbal medicines, particularly widely used for the treatment of depression, anxiety, and unrest—a "mood enhancer" as I read on one of the bottles. At one time it also found medicinal use among the Iroquois and Cherokee. The drug fell into disuse and was nearly forgotten until the twentieth century when a tea prepared from it proved effective as a nerve tonic in Europe (Tyler, 1993). *Time* magazine (April 20, 2001, p. 60) reported that the

St.-John's-wort, *Hypericum perforatum*, called "*Hypericum*, S. Iohns wort," by Gerard

most definitive study on St.-John's-wort to date failed to show that it had any effect in controlling depression. As pointed out in two letters to the magazine (May 21), the subjects tested in the study suffered from major depression and the herb might still be effective for mild depression.

The plant is not a serious weed in most of the United States, and in fact, in most places it is thought of as a wildflower rather than as a weed. However, it has become an obnoxious weed in Australia and the western United States, and it is known as Klamath weed in the Northwest, probably named after the Klamath River of southern Oregon and northern California. It is not easy to eradicate. It is also poisonous to livestock.

Commelinaceae Spiderwort Family

Herbs with jointed stems; leaves alternate, parallel-veined; stem sheathing at the base; petals three, colored; sepals three, usually green; fruit a small capsule. Some species of the family, particularly spiderwort (*Tradescantia*), are cultivated as ornamentals.

Dayflower *Commelina communis*

The Names. Dayflower is a misnomer for the petals seldom last more than a few hours. Linnaeus dedicated the genus to the brothers Commelin, two of whom became well known botanically and are represented by the two large petals, and a third who did not, represented by the small petal; *communis* means "growing in colonies."

The Time and Place. Summer. Native to Asia.

The Description. Somewhat sprawling annual; leaves slightly fleshy, lance-shaped, to four inches long and about half as wide, the uppermost leaves folded over the flower buds; flowers irregular because of the different-shaped petals and anthers, the two larger petals blue and the third paler to white.

The Virtues. The only virtues that I know of is that dayflower is not a particularly obnoxious weed and is rather attractive when the flowers are open.

Convolvulaceae Morning Glory Family

Chiefly climbing or trailing herbaceous vines; leaves alternate; flowers showy, of five united petals with two bracts beneath them; few-seeded capsular fruits; some members contain a milky juice. In addition to a very important food plant, the sweet potato (*Ipomoea batatas*), this family contains a number of plants grown as ornamentals. Some morning glories are hallucinogenic, and one species enjoyed considerable popularity as such on college campuses a number of years ago. Although the dodders (*Cuscuta*) are parasitic, nongreen plants, and are sometimes placed in a family of their own (Cuscutaceae), I am including them here for convenience, for in many books they are included in the morning glory family.

Hedge Bindweed, Greater Bindweed, or Wild Morning Glory *Calystegia sepium*

The Names. Bindweed because in its viny growth it binds other plants. *Calystegia* is Greek, meaning "beautiful covering"; *sepium* is Latin and means "of hedges." In most older books, hedge bindweed is given as *Convolvulus sepium*.

The Time and Place. Mid- to late summer. It has generally been thought to be from Eurasia, but apparently there are both native and introduced forms in the northeastern United States.

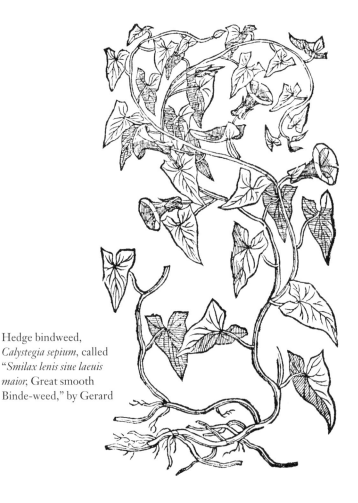

Hedge bindweed, *Calystegia sepium*, called "*Smilax lenis siue laeuis maior*, Great smooth Binde-weed," by Gerard

The Description. Twining perennial with arrowhead-shaped leaves, long-stalked; flowers white or pink, one and a half to three inches long with two stigmas; beneath the flowers are two leafy bracts that cover the buds and, later, the base of the flowers.

The Virtues. Bailey (1949) lists this bindweed as a cultivated ornamental plant under the name Rutland beauty. I have heard of people transplanting the weed to their garden because of the attractive flowers. I imagine that later some of them may have regretted it.

Field Bindweed *Convolvulus arvensis*
PLATE 16

The Names. For bindweed see the previous entry on hedge bindweed. *Convolvulus* comes from the Latin *convolvere*, to entwine; *arvensis* means "of fields."

The Time and Place. Mid- to late summer. From Europe.

The Description. Field bindweed is similar to hedge bindweed but the flowers are much smaller and the two minute bracts are a little distance from the flower.

The Virtues. Except for the attractive flowers I know of none. Gerard says that most of the bindweeds "are not fit for medicine, but vnprofitable weeds, and hurtfull vnto each thing that groweth next vnto them." He was certainly correct, at least for the last part, for today *Convolvulus arvensis* is regarded as one of the world's worst weeds (Holm et al., 1977). It reproduces by seed as well as vegetatively. Even very small pieces of the underground parts can give rise to new plants, making the plant difficult to control.

Dodder, Love Vine, or Strangle Vine *Cuscuta pentagona*

The Names. Dodder is of uncertain origin; love vine because it is entangling and suffocating; strangle vine because it kills the plants on which it grows by strangling them. This species is also called field dodder. *Cuscuta* is of Arabic origin and its meaning is unknown; *pentagona* means five-angled, probably referring to the calyx or corolla.

The Time and Place. Summer. Native to much of North America.

The Description. Leafless annuals; stems usually orange; flowers small, white.

The Virtues. The dodders are all parasites and hence have few, if any, virtues. Some of them parasitize other weeds but many of them attack crop plants. I do not remember all the host plants in my garden, but I do recall that in some years they grew on clover. Fortunately, they never occurred on any of our experimental crop plants. In Europe the native species were used in medicine, and they were once popular in the treatment of jaundice. The American species were also used medicinally by the Indians. Two of the common names in England are worth mentioning—devil's guts and devil's thread—the devil spun the dodder at night to destroy clover. The seeds of dodder germinate on the ground, and soon the young plants attach themselves to other plants by means of suckers through which they derive their nourishment from their host.

Morning Glory *Ipomoea hederacea* and *I. purpurea*

The Names. The attractive flower, open in the morning, is responsible for the common name. The name morning glory apparently was first used for the bindweeds and then transferred to the ipomoeas. *Ipomoea* is from the Greek *ips*, a worm, and *homoios*, resembling, because of its twining or crawling. Bailey (1949) says the name is of no particular significance. *Hederacea* means resembling *Hedera* (English ivy) because the lobed leaves suggest that plant, from which we also get the common name ivy-leaf morning glory. *Purpurea* is purple, referring to one of the flower colors. *Ipomoea purpurea* is also called common morning glory.

The Time and Place. Late summer. Both species are from warmer regions of the Americas.

The Description. Morning glories have a single head-shaped or lobed stigma in the center of the flower, which is one of the best ways to distinguish them from the bindweeds. Both species are annual vines, trailing on the ground or climbing other plants in my garden, and have showy flowers, usually blue, purple, or white. The common morning glory (*Ipomoea purpurea*) has flowers more than two inches long and unlobed, heart-shaped leaves whereas the ivy-leaf morning glory (*I. hederacea*) has flowers about two inches long and three-lobed leaves.

The Virtues. Both common and ivy-leaf morning glory are grown for their flowers, and escapes from cultivation were the source of weeds of the common sort. Michael Clegg and collaborators have made studies of the flowers of this species and, among other things, found that there are eight different color types. Pollinators, chiefly bumblebees, tend to avoid the white ones in favor of the other colors. Gerard, after mentioning the medicinal virtues, including "it driues out all kinde of wormes," tells us that "it troubleth the belly, and causeth a readinesse to vomit" as well as "worketh slowly, . . . wherefore we thinke good to passe it ouer."

Cucurbitaceae Gourd Family

Mostly somewhat succulent herbs, climbing by means of tendrils; leaves simple, often lobed; flowers bisexual or unisexual, the petals usually five, free or partially united, white, yellow, or greenish, the ovary borne below other flower parts; fruits fleshy or dry, one- to many-seeded. Most members of the gourd family are native to warmer regions. Economically, it is a very important family and includes pumpkins, squashes, and ornamental gourds (*Cucurbita*), watermelon (*Citrullus*), cucumber and various melons (*Cucumis*), the bottle or hard-shelled gourd (*Lagenaria*), and loofah gourds (*Luffa*).

Bur Cucumber *Sicyos angulatus*

The Names. The fruit is bur-like in that it is covered with prickles. *Sicyos* is a Greek name for cucumber; *angulatus* refers to the angled or lobed leaves.

The Time and Place. Summer. Native to eastern North America.

The Description. Climbing annual plants with broad, three- or five-lobed leaves; flowers small, whitish; fruits clustered, one-seeded, not splitting open at maturity and covered with barbed, prickly bristles; all parts with soft, clammy hairs.

The Virtues. Probably none except that it belongs to the gourd family, which is important to me as will be explained. The bristles on the fruit make *Sicyos angulatus* rather objectionable. Deam (1940) points out that they will penetrate clothing and that "in husking corn the hands of workmen are injured." We can be happy that the plant is not as objectionable as it once was, for very few people husk corn today. The farm combine has all but eliminated that task.

A few weeks before the manuscript was completed, I thought that this book would have to go to press without the gourd family being represented. That would have been a tragedy for it is one of my favorite families and I would not have an excuse to mention *The Gourd Book*, whose author is Charles Heiser (1979). Just in time I discovered a plant of bur cucumber in the experimental field, growing with my gourds. Dave Campbell, who is in charge of our field operations, told me that he thought that the plant grew there in earlier years but that I had failed to see it. In several places I have pointed out that plants we grew for study at the field later became weeds there. For many years I grew bottle gourds (*Lagenaria siceraria*) and ornamental gourds (*Cucurbita pepo*) at the field. I expected that one or the other, or both, might become volunteers there, but neither did. I was particularly interested in the latter for some people thought that the wild gourds that occur in some of the southern states are weedy descendents of escaped ornamental gourds. It is now thought that these wild gourds are remnants of populations of ancient wild gourds and that they gave rise to some of the domesticated squashes (*C. pepo*) in eastern North America in prehistoric time. Other squashes of the same species were domesticated independently in Mexico ten thousand years ago, making it the oldest domesticated plant in the Americas (Smith, 1995).

Cyperaceae Sedge Family

Grass-like plants but with solid, often triangular stems; usually found in wet places. In spite of its large size, the sedge family provides us with very few economic plants. Papyrus (*Cyperus papyrus*) was the plant used for making paper in ancient Egypt and today is widely grown as an ornamental. The *totora* (*Schoeno-plectus californicus*), a bulrush, is used to make the boats seen on Lake Titicaca.

False Nutsedge *Cyperus strigosus*

The Names. The common name comes from Gleason and Cronquist (1991); most authors don't give one. The true nutsedges are species of *Cyperus* with small, edible, nut-like tubers. *Cyperus* is the ancient Greek name; *strigosus,* Latin for "bearing stiff hairs," was adopted by Linnaeus for this species. Why, I am not sure, but he cites an earlier author who had referred to the flower spikes as being strigose.

The Time and Place. Summer. Native to much of North America.

The Description. Perennial from less than an inch to three feet tall; stems triangular from an enlarged hard base; flowering clusters golden yellow, borne on umbrella-like rays or stalks. This description will hardly serve to distinguish *Cyperus strigosus* from many other sedges.

The Virtues. Its chief virtue is that it is not a serious weed in my garden, appearing only in small numbers. I counted only five plants there on my last census. One member of the genus, yellow nutsedge or chufa (*Cyperus esculentus*), which is one of the world's worst weeds (Holm et al., 1977), does occur in Indiana but has never appeared in my garden; this species is sometimes cultivated for the edible tubers. Many years ago I recall hoeing out another weedy sedge, but I never identified it. At the time I didn't know that I would be writing this book.

Dipsacaceae Teasel Family

Herbs with opposite, or rarely whorled, leaves; flowers small, aggregated into dense heads surrounded by bracts, petals four or five, partially united, the ovary borne below the other flower parts. A few members of the teasel family are grown as ornamentals. The dried heads of fuller's teasel (*Dipsacus fullonum*), with their recurved tipped bracts, are used to raise the nap on woolen cloth.

Teasel *Dipsacus sylvestris*

The Names. Teazel, as it has been spelled in England, is from the Anglo-Saxon *taesel*, meaning to tease cloth. *Dipsacus*, the Greek name for teasel, comes from *dipsa*, thirst, for the united leaf bases of some species collect rainwater. The water from these was once thought to have special medicinal properties. *Sylvestris* means "of the woods," not very appropriate for the species nearly always occurs in open places.

The Time and Place. Mid- to late summer. From Europe.

The Description. Biennial, two to four feet tall, prickly; leaf pairs grown together at their bases; flowers in a dense head; individual flowers long, slender, and tubular, whitish with purple lobes. These plants are often thought to be some kind of a thistle by nonbotanists, and indeed, Gerard includes teasel with the thistles.

The Virtues. As Gerard tells us, "there is small vse of Teasell in medicines." The "rootes . . . have a certaine cleaning facultie" and had some medicinal use. This species is of no value in the wool industry for the spines on the head are straight rather than hooked as in fuller's teasel. The dried heads, however, are good

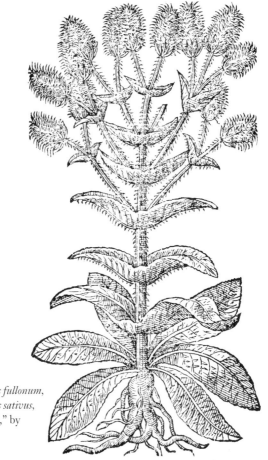

Teasel, *Dipsacus fullonum,* called "*Dipsacus sativus,* Garden Teasell," by Gerard

for winter flower arrangements. In some more recent books, *Dipsacus sylvestris* is considered to be only a race of fuller's teasel.

Euphorbiaceae Spurge Family

Herbs, shrubs, and trees, some cactus-like; juice often milky; leaves usually alternate and with stipules; flowers with or without sepals and petals, the ovary usually with three cavities. The spurge family is very diverse and of considerable economic importance; it includes yuca, cassava, and manioc (*Manihot esculenta*), a basic food plant in the tropics but little known in the United States except in the form of tapioca; *Hevea brasiliensis*, the best source of natural rubber; the castor bean (*Ricinus communis*); and many ornamentals, prominent among them poinsettia (*Euphorbia pulcherrima*), crown-of-thorns (*E. milii*), and croton (*Codiaeum variegatum*).

Spurge *Euphorbia*

The Names. Spurge comes from the Old French *espurge*, "purging plant." *Euphorbia* was named for Euphorbus, physician to Juba, a king of Numidia (now Algeria). Four species have been found in my garden: (1) *Euphorbia nutans* (nodding), nodding spurge because the stems are usually nodding; also called milk spurge and eyebane (poison to the eye). (2) *Euphorbia maculata* (spotted), spotted spurge because the leaves sometimes have a dark spot; also called creeping spurge and milk purslane. (3) *Euphorbia dentata* (toothed), toothed spurge because of the toothed leaves. (4) *Euphorbia cyathophora* (cup-bearing), painted spurge and fire-on-the-mountain, so called because the upper leaves are red at the base.

The Time and Place. Mid- to late summer. *Euphorbia nutans, E. maculata,* and *E. dentata* are native to eastern North America; *E. cyathophora* is native to the southern United States and tropical America. Only *E. nutans* now occurs in my garden; it has been several years since I have seen the others there.

The Description. The flower structure of the spurges is rather complicated. What appears to the uninitiated to be a single flower is in reality a collection of individual male flowers and a single female flower grouped together in a small cup. At its summit the cup bears one to five glands, and sometimes the glands have small petal-like appendages. Magnification is necessary to make out the details, and the poinsettia, which has much larger flowers than these weeds, would be a good place to start. All the spurges have a milky juice and capsular fruits. These weedy species are all annuals. *Euphorbia nutans* and *E. maculata* have four glands on the cups, with petaloid appendages and mostly opposite leaves with stipules, whereas *E. dentata* and *E. cyathophora* have fewer glands (usually one) and lack petaloid appendages and stipules.

(1) *Euphorbia nutans* is one to two feet tall with erect or ascending, nodding stems; the stems and capsules are smooth. (2) *Euphorbia maculata* is smaller, often prostrate and forming mats; the stem (at least when young) and the capsule bear many short hairs. Both the first and this second species sometimes have dark spots on the leaves and are now placed in the genus *Chamaesyce* in some books. (3) *Euphorbia dentata* reaches heights of two feet; the leaves are mostly opposite, often with hairs. (4) *Euphorbia cyathophora* is often taller than *E. dentata;* leaves are mostly alternate, lack hairs, and are quite variable in shape, from very narrow to fiddle-shaped, the upper ones often blotched with red.

The Virtues. A number of the spurges were used in Indian medicine. I learned from my grandfather that the milky juice could be used to remove warts, and I found that it was successful. (At other times I have had warts disappear using nothing at all.) I have also since learned that the milky juice can cause dermatitis in some people. The spurges are not recommended for eating.

Fabaceae Pea or Bean Family

Mostly herbs; leaves alternate, with stipules, and usually composed of leaflets; petals five, separate, usually of different shapes, often giving a butterfly-like appearance to the flower, the stamens ten, frequently united by filaments in various ways; fruit a dry one- to many-seeded pod, usually splitting on two sides at maturity. The very large pea or bean family, also called the Leguminosae, is one of the most important as far as human welfare is concerned. It includes a number of food plants—many kinds of beans and peas, lentils, and peanuts, and forage plants such as clover and alfalfa—and many ornamentals—wisteria, lupine, and many more.

Considering the size of the family, I am surprised that it includes so few weeds. Alfalfa and several clovers sometimes escape from cultivation and can be classed as weeds. In addition to including so many important plants, the pea or bean family is also of great significance in that most members are able to fix atmospheric nitrogen through the action of bacteria living in nodules on their roots. Thus a great many legumes can increase soil fertility.

Some years ago I planted kudzu (*Pueraria montana*) in my garden, wanting to have plants to show my students. Although I was aware that this plant could take over whole fields in the South, I thought that we were too far north in Bloomington for it to pose any danger. It spread rapidly, however, and I realized that it would have to be removed. Cutting it to the ground several times during the year did nothing to dampen its enthusiasm for life, so finally I had to spend several hours digging out all of the roots, which finally eliminated it. It is now listed as an invasive plant in Indiana (Anonymous, 2000). For more, see "Kudzu: love it—or run," by Doug Stewart (2000).

Japanese Clover and Korean Clover *Kummerowia striata* and *K. stipulacea*

The Names. The true clovers belong to genus *Trifolium*, but many other genera resembling them are also called clovers. Japanese clover (*Kummerowia striata*) and Korean clover (*K. stipulacea*) come from the countries after which they were named. *Kummerowia* commemorates J. Kummerow, a Polish botanist; *striata* means striate, or having parallel lines (on the leaflets), and *stipulacea* means having stipules. Both species are often commonly called lespedeza instead of clover; at one time both were placed in the genus *Lespedeza*. This name honors Vicente Manuel de Céspedes, the Spanish governor of Florida in the late eighteenth century; the name was misspelled as Léspedez. Several native perennial species of *Lespedeza* occur in Indiana and are called bush clovers.

The Time and Place. Late summer. From Asia.

The Description. Small, usually erect, annuals; leaflets three; corollas pinkish, pods one-seeded, not splitting open at maturity. The stem hairs in Japanese clover (*Kummerowia striata*) are bent downward whereas in Korean clover (*K. stipulacea*) they are bent upward. One needs a lens to make out the difference.

The Virtues. These species were originally introduced as forage plants. Both make excellent food for livestock and also improve soil fertility. Around Bloomington they occur naturally in rather poor soil. Both *Kummerowia striata* and *K. stipulacea* were in the garden before we intentionally planted Japanese clover in some bare areas there. Deam (1940) points out that these species had spread with remarkable rapidity in Indiana in the early part of the twentieth century.

Black Medic or Nonesuch *Medicago lupulina*

The Names. *Medice*, from which we get the common and genus names, is the Greek name for alfalfa (*Medicago sativa*). *Medice* in turn comes from Media (now in Iran), the country where alfalfa originated. Black, I suppose, comes from the black pod of *M. lupulina*; *lupulina* means hop-like. I have never heard the name nonesuch used. It comes from England and apparently refers to the plant's superiority as fodder, a name that probably more properly belongs to alfalfa, which is a superior plant for fodder.

The Time and Place. Early summer. From Eurasia.

The Description. Rather small, decumbent or prostrate annuals or biennials; leaflets three, toothed; flowers yellow, in dense clusters; pod sometimes coiled, one-seeded, becoming black.

The Virtues. Black medic has been used as a fodder plant, but its greatest claim to fame may be that it is a relative of alfalfa. According to Mrs. Dana (1993), a "Dr. Prior says that for many years this plant has been recognized in Ireland as the true shamrock."

White Sweet Clover and Yellow Sweet Clover
Melilotus albus and *M. officinalis*

The Names. Sweet because of the fragrance of the newly mown plants; clover because of its resemblance to true clover (*Trifolium*). The word clover is from the Old English *clafre*. The colors, white (*Melilotus albus*) or yellow (*M. officinalis*), refer to the flowers. *Melilotus* comes from the Greek *meli*, honey, and *lotus*, an ancient name often used for clover-like plants. (Melilot is a common name derived from that of the genus that is sometimes used for these species.) *Albus* translates as white, *officinalis* as official, "used in medicine."

The Time and Place. Midsummer. Both species from Eurasia.

The Description. Biennial or annual, two to four feet tall; leaflets three, finely toothed; flowers on short stalks in an elongate or spike-like arrangement; pods one- or two-seeded, usually not splitting open at maturity. The two species, distinguished by the color of the flowers, have long been recognized by botanists but in some more recent works they are considered to constitute only one species, *Melilotus officinalis*.

The Virtues. The sweet clovers have a number of virtues. They have been important in medicine and are still in some favor for this purpose. Gerard cites six ways in which they were so used, and I quote the first one:

> Melilote boiled in sweet wine vntill it be soft, if you adde thereto the yolke of a rosted egge, the meale of Fenegreeke and Lineseed, the roots of March Mallowes and hogs greace stamped together, and vsed as a pultis or cataplasma, plaisterwise, doth asswage and soften all

manner of swellings, especially about the matrix, fundament and genitories, being applied vnto those places hot.

I find a few uses listed for the Indians: among the Navajo it was
used for colds caused by being chilled. The fragrance of the plants
on drying is from coumarin, a chemical found in sweet clovers
and a number of other plants. It is largely responsible for the odor
of the new-mown hay and is widely used in perfumery and for
flavoring tobacco. The flowers of sweet clover were once used as
flavoring in cheese, and the leaves were packed with stored furs to
impart a pleasant odor and to protect against moths.

Both *Melilotus albus* and *M. officinalis* were once important
forage plants but are little used today, for they are inferior to
alfalfa (*Medicago sativa*) in this regard. The plants are excellent
for soil improvement. They are both fine bee plants and are said
to be intentionally planted for the purpose. I didn't know the
seeds could be used for human food until I read Jones's (1991)
account. She uses the seeds, whole or ground, in soups, stews,
and cookies. However, Duke (1992) states that the seeds are
reported to poison horses. I was surprised to see these species on
the list of invasive species in Indiana (Anonymous, 2000) for I
don't think of them as bad weeds and have never seen them
invade natural areas.

Geraniaceae Geranium Family

Mostly herbs; leaves usually lobed or deeply divided, with stipules; petals five, separate, the stamens usually ten. This family
includes a number of ornamentals, of which the geranium is the
best known. It, however, is not now a member of the genus
Geranium but instead is placed in *Pelargonium*.

Carolina Cranesbill *Geranium carolinianum*

The Names. The long, beaked fruit has the appearance of a crane's bill and gives us both the common and scientific names, *Geranium* being an old Greek name from *geranos*, crane.

The Time and Place. Late spring. Native to much of North America.

The Description. Annual; one to three feet tall; stems hairy; leaves opposite, cleft into five to nine segments, which are deeply toothed or lobed; petals inconspicuous, pale pink; fruit (the crane's bill) one-half to nearly an inch long, splitting into five parts at maturity, each part coiling backward to eject the seeds.

The Virtues. I know of none. Our native weedy cranesbill, *Geranium carolinianum*, is far less famous than herb Robert (*G. robertianum*), rare in Indiana but widespread in the Old World and now in parts of North America. It does not occur in my garden, which is just as well, for the explanation of its name is most complicated.

Lamiaceae Mint Family

Members of the Lamiaceae, or Labiatae, often have a square stem and a minty odor, and when one or the other of these is lacking, they can be easily recognized by the flowers. The five-lobed corolla is nearly always two-lipped, the stamens are four or two, and the fruit is made up of four small nutlets. The leaves are simple and opposite. The mint family is of economic importance because of its large number of ornamentals and aromatic herbs, including basil, horehound, lavender, marjoram, peppermint, rosemary, sage, savory, spearmint, and thyme.

Ground Ivy or Gill-over-the-Ground *Glechoma hederacea*

The Names. The plant creeps over the ground like ivy, hence the first name. Gill is said to come from the French *guiller*, to ferment beer, for ground ivy was used by early Saxons to clear their beer before hops came into use. Gill also, of course, means girl. Many given names have been used for this plant, such as creeping Charlie and run-away-robin. Another name for it is alehoof (see below). *Glechoma* is an old Greek name for pennyroyal (*Mentha pulegium*), another mint; *hederacea* means ivy-like.

The Time and Place. Late spring. From Europe.

The Description. Creeping perennials with stalked, roundish toothed leaves usually less than an inch in diameter; flowers in the axils of upper leaves, bluish purple, the upper pair of stamens longer than the lower pair, the calyx with fifteen nerves or veins; crushed leaves with balsamic odor.

The Virtues. Gerard, after telling us that it was good for ringing in the ears, ulcers, sciatica, yellow jaundice, and inflammation of the eyes, writes that "the women in our Northern parts . . . do tunne the herb Ale-hoof into their Ale, but the reason thereof I know not." Ground ivy is still a popular home remedy, particularly as a tea for coughs and a snuff for headaches. The plant was used medicinally by the Cherokee. A variegated form is sometimes grown as an ornamental ground cover.

Henbit and Purple Dead Nettle *Lamium amplexicaule* and *L. purpureum*

The Names. Why henbit (hen's bite, *Lamium amplexicaule*) I do not know. Perhaps chickens eat the plant, but I suspect that it is

because the plant was once thought to be related to chickweed—
Gerard places it with his Bastard Chickweeds. Purple dead nettle (*L. purpureum*) is more readily explained: nettle because of
some resemblance to the leaves of true nettles (members of a
different family, the Urticaceae), and dead, meaning without the

Purple dead nettle,
Lamium purpureum,
called "*Lamium
Pannonicum, siue Galeopsis,*
Hungary dead Nettle,"
by Gerard

stinging hairs of some nettles. *Lamium* is a Latin name for a net-tle-like plant; *amplexicaule* means clasping, referring to the leaves clasping the stems, and *purpureum* means purple.

The Time and Place. Early spring. Both species from Eurasia.

The Description. Rather short or decumbent annuals with some-what heart-shaped, double-toothed leaves; flowers clustered in the axils of the leaves, calyx five-nerved. Henbit (*Lamium amplexicaule*) has sessile, clasping leaves, six to ten flowers in each cluster, pink or purplish corolla, and a calyx about one-fourth of an inch long. Purple dead nettle (*L. purpureum*) has stalked, deeper green or purplish leaves, three to seven flowers in each cluster, purplish corolla, and frequently a slightly longer calyx. Neither species has any minty odor that I can detect.

The Virtues. Both henbit (*Lamium amplexicaule*) and purple dead nettle (*L. purpureum*) have been used as potherbs and in medi-cine. Gerard writes,

> the floures [of dead nettle] are baked with sugar as roses
> are, . . . as also the distilled water of them, which is vsed
> to make the heart merry; to make good colour in the
> face, and to make the vitall spirits more fresh and liuely.

Self-Heal or Heal-All *Prunella vulgaris*

The Names. Self-heal and heal-all come from the plant's use in medicine. It was the reputed cure for a number of ailments. Although Fernald (1950) states that *Prunella* is of uncertain ori-gin, Bailey (1949) and others say that this name comes from the German *Bräune*, quinsy, a disease of the throat, for which it was used as a remedy. (It was once spelled *Brunella*.) *Vulgaris* is Latin for common.

The Time and Place. Summer. Widespread in the northern hemisphere. We have the native race, widespread in North America, as well as the European race.

The Description. Prostrate to nearly erect perennial from a few inches to two feet tall; flowers crowded into a short spike, blue to

Self-heal, *Prunella vulgaris,*
called "*Prunella,* Selfe-heale,"
by Gerard

purple, rarely white or pink, the upper stamens shorter than the lower, the calyx deeply two-lipped, the upper three lobes differ- ent from the lower two; leaves with stalks, lance-shaped to ovate; lacking a minty odor.

The Virtues. Gerard had high praise for "Prunell," a decoction of which "made with wine or water, doth ioine together and make whole and sound all wounds, ..." The plant is still much used in herbal medicine, particularly as an astringent, in an infusion as a gargle for sore throat, and as a tonic for general strengthening. *Prunella vulgaris* has also been grown as an ornamental.

Lauraceae Laurel Family

Aromatic trees and shrubs with alternate leaves; flowers small, lacking petals, the anthers opening by uplifting valves. Economi- ically, the most important species of the laurel family are avo- cado (*Persea americana*), cinnamon (*Cinnamomum zeylanicum*), and laurel (*Laurus nobilis*).

Sassafras *Sassafras albidum*
PLATE 17

The Names. Few plants have only one common name, but I know of but one for this species, and it is the same as the genus. My sources disagree as to its origin. Fernald (1950) states that sassafras is "the aboriginal name, applied by the early French settlers in Florida" whereas Bailey (1949) states that "Sassafras is Spanish *salsafras* or *Saxifraga*, supposed to have similar medici- nal properties." *Albidum* means whitish, apparently from the color of the roots. (Some botanists recognize two varieties, one white, the other red.) The name sassafras is also applied to several other aromatic trees, unrelated to our species.

The Time and Place. Early summer. Native to the eastern United States.

The Description. Usually small trees but at times reaching 125 feet; leaves quite variable—unlobed, two-lobed (mitten-shaped), and three-lobed leaves frequently found on the same plant—crushed leaves very aromatic with rather pleasant odor but not at all like the odor of the roots; fruits blue, fleshy, one-seeded. Of course, not all trees bear fruits for this is a species in which the male and female flowers are borne on separate plants.

The Virtues. In Indiana, where I know it best, sassafras invades old, abandoned fields and sometimes fills the area. It spreads readily by root shoots to form colonies. However, in most places, at least, it does no harm as a weed but rather contributes to re-forestation. It has many other virtues as well, not the least of which is that its fall colors—reds and oranges—are some of the best in the flora. For that reason I decided it would be desirable to have one in my yard, but it took considerable effort, for they do not transplant well, and only on my fourth try was I successful.

Sassafras has been much used in medicine and early was considered the most important medicinal plant of North America—it was thought to be a panacea. Tons of it were shipped to Europe and it was an early export from the English colony at Jamestown. As it did not cure everything that it was supposed to, it gradually fell out of favor. However, it continues to be important in folk medicine. I heard about roots of sassafras being used for tea and as a flavoring as a boy and have drunk the tea on many occasions with pleasure. Some people drink it the year around but others use it only in the spring. My grandmother told me that after a cold winter, one's blood grows thick, and the best way to thin it is with sassafras tea. The tea reportedly cures a number of other ailments.

Not only did the Indians use it for medicine but also for food. The leaves, which are very mucilaginous, are used as gumbo to thicken soup. The oil from various parts of the plant is also used to flavor dentrifices, root beer, and candies. A few years ago it was found that the oil, safrole, caused cancer in rodents, and since that time its use in root beer has been forbidden by law. The wood also has a number of uses and is particularly good for fence posts.

Liliaceae Lily Family

Mostly perennial herbs with narrow, parallel-veined leaves; flowers usually with six petal-like segments, six stamens, and a single three-locular ovary; fruit a capsule, rarely a berry. The lily family includes food plants—onions, garlic, leeks, and related species (*Allium*), and asparagus (*Asparagus officinale*)—a large number of ornamentals, including species of lily (*Lilium*), tulip (*Tulipa*), and narcissus (*Narcissus*), and several medicinal plants.

Garlic *Allium canadense* and *A. vineale*

The Names. The word garlic is from the Old English *garleac*, spear leek. The name wild garlic or meadow garlic is used for *Allium canadense* and field garlic or crow garlic for *A. vineale*, although many people call both of them wild garlic or sometimes wild onion. *Allium* is the ancient Latin name for garlic; *vineale* means "of vineyards."

The Time and Place. Early summer. *Allium canadense* is native to eastern North America, and *A. vineale* is from Europe (as is our cultivated garlic, *A. sativa*).

The Description. These species have the strong odor of garlic and the characteristic bulb, the enlarged edible underground

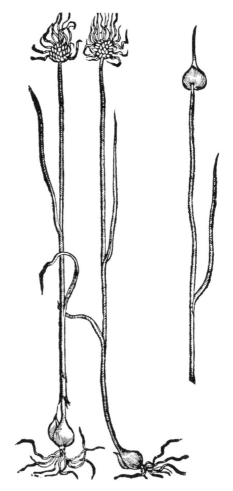

Field garlic or crow garlic, *Allium vineale*, called "*Allium syluestre*, Crow Garlicke," by Gerard

structure. In both, the flowers are often replaced by small bulbs. *Allium canadense* has flattened, solid leaves whereas those of *A. vineale* are nearly round and hollow. If flowers are present, those of the former species are white or pink whereas those of the latter are red or pink, rarely white or greenish.

The Virtues. Our native species, *Allium canadense*, is said to be very good for eating, but field garlic (*A. vineale*) is too strong for most people. My grandfather hated the latter because cows would eat it and when they did so it would give the milk the strong odor and taste of garlic. As a result he would be unable to sell the milk. Deam (1940) calls it "one of the most pernicious weeds in southern Indiana." The replacement of seeds by small bulbs apparently has contributed to the success of both species as weeds. The Indians used both in medicine in several ways, including rubbing the plant on the body to protect against insect bites and snakebites. Cultivated garlic (*A. sativa*) has even more medicinal uses than either of the other two. It is hard to escape the advertisements on the radio for one of the commercial preparations.

Orange Daylily or Tawny Daylily *Hemerocallis fulva*
PLATE 18

The Names. Both the common name and the genus name come from the short-lived flowers, which are open only for one day. *Hemera* is Greek for day and *callos* for beauty, hence beauty for a day; *fulva* is Latin for reddish yellow. Lily is from *Lilium*, the classical and modern name for true lilies.

The Time and Place. Early to midsummer. From Eurasia.

The Description. Perennial, two to three feet tall, from tuberous roots and underground stems; leaves long and narrow, all from the base of the plant; flowers large, lily-like, tawny orange; plants sterile.

The Virtues. This species and several other members of the genus were introduced into North America as ornamentals for their showy flowers. Only the orange daylily (*Hemerocallis fulva*) has become widely naturalized, although the yellow daylily (*H. lilioasphodelus*) occasionally is found as an escape from cultivation. The orange daylily has long been a popular food in Japan and China, and more recently in the United States. The fresh or dried flowers and the tuberous roots are the parts used. Not a single book insofar as I am aware has mentioned any toxic effects, so it was with some surprise that I heard of the experience of Florence Wagner. She taught a course in wild food plants at the University of Michigan and at the conclusion of the course a banquet was held, consisting of dishes prepared from wild foods. After the banquet one year, several of the students became violently ill. Fortunately, there was no lasting damage. Dr. Wagner determined to find the culprit among the plants so she had the students give her a list of the foods they had eaten. All the students who became ill had eaten daylily whereas none of the others had partaken of it. After that experience, she never taught the course again.

Star-of-Bethlehem or Nap-at-Noon
Ornithogalum umbellatum
PLATE 19

The Names. Gerard uses the name "Starre of Bethlehem" but he does not tell us why. The flower is six-pointed and could be imagined to resemble a star. Many of the other names—nap-at-noon, sleepy Dick, ten o'clock lady, Betty-go-to-bed-at-noon, and several others—are used because the flowers close early in the day. *Ornithogalum*, according to Fernald (1950), is "a whimsical name" from the Greek, meaning bird's milk; *umbellatum* refers to the nature of the flower clusters, all of which have stalks that are attached at the same level.

Star-of-Bethlehem, *Ornithogalum umbellatum*, called "*Ornithogalum*, Star of Bethlehem," by Gerard

The Time and Place. Late April and May. From Europe.

The Description. Plants about six inches tall from odorless bulbs; leaves many from the base of the plant, very narrow, and with a white longitudinal line on the surface; flowers of six petal-like structures, white above and with a green stripe beneath, about an inch across, usually five to seven flowers to a stalk.

The Virtues. Gerard found no virtues for the plant. Nor have I except that the flowers are attractive. (It was originally introduced into North America as an ornamental.) Deam (1940) states that it "crowds out all other vegetation and where it is found it should be exterminated at once." It is now given on the invasive plant list for Indiana (Anonymous, 2000). The cooked bulbs have been used as famine food, but they are reported to be poisonous to livestock, and children have been poisoned by eating the flowers as well as bulbs. The leaves of the plant are some of the earliest to emerge in the late winter or early spring and one would expect it to be among the first to flower, but it usually waits until mid-May in the area of Bloomington to do so, long after many of the other spring flowers have gone to fruit.

Malvaceae Mallow Family

Mostly herbs with alternate leaves with stipules; petals five, the sepals often with sepal-like structures or bracts beneath them, the stamens many, with their stalks (filaments) united below; fruit dry at maturity, a capsule or splitting into segments. Cotton (*Gossypium*) is the member of the mallow family with the greatest economic importance. The family also includes a number of ornamentals of which hollyhock (*Althaea rosea*) and several species of *Hibiscus* are the best known. Gumbo or okra (*Abelmoschus esculentus*), grown for its edible fruit, also belongs here.

Velvetleaf, Butter Print, or Piemarker
Abutilon theophrasti

The Names. Velvetleaf is very apt for the hairs on the leaf give it a velvety feel. Butter print and piemarker come from the use of the fruits to press attractive designs into butter or dough. Or so I had heard, but recently when using the pods to make prints in butter (illustrating the lengths to which I have gone in my research for this book), I found the results very disappointing. The pods were not rigid enough. So back to the books and I found that Spencer (1957) notes that the pods "look very much like the print blocks used by farm housewives for stamping their rolls of butter." *Abutilon*, the meaning of which is unknown, is an ancient name, apparently of Arabic origin; *theophrasti* honors the famous pre-Christian Greek scientist, Theophrastus.

The Time and Place. Summer. From southern Asia.

Piemarker, *Abutilon theophrasti*, fruit, ×1.5, drawing by Marilyn Rudd

The Description. Annual, two to five feet tall with broad, velvety, heart-shaped, angular leaves, four to six inches long; flowers yellow, rather small; no bracts subtending the sepals; ripe fruit hairy, dry, separating into ten to fifteen parts, each with two or more seeds.

The Virtues. In cutting the stems, one finds that they are very tough. The fibers responsible for the toughness were once used in China for making rugs and paper. And when was the last time you were served butter with prints on it? Several members of the genus *Abutilon* have more attractive flowers than this species and are grown as ornamentals.

Prickly Sida or Prickly Mallow *Sida spinosa*

The Names. The plants have a small prickle or spiny structure at the base of the leaves. *Sida* is a name used by Theophrastus for some related plant; *spinosa* means spiny.

The Time and Place. Mid- to late summer. Probably native to tropical America.

The Description. Annual, one to three feet tall with long-stalked, oblong to ovate leaves with a small spine-like process at the base of the leaf stalk; flowers pale yellow, small; no bracts subtending the calyx; ripe fruit splitting into five segments.

The Virtues. None of which I am aware. *Sida spinosa* is not a serious weed but a related tropical species (*S. acuta*), one of the world's worst weeds (Holm et al., 1977), is found in the southern United States.

Menispermaceae Moonseed Family

Twining, woody vines; flowers small, unisexual, whitish or greenish; fruits fleshy, one-seeded.

Moonseed or Yellow Parilla *Menispermum canadense*

The Names. The common name is a translation of the genus name, from the Greek *men*, moon, and *sperm*, seed, so called because of the crescent shape of the seed. I have never heard the other common name used but some books give it. I don't know its origin. Gerard says that it means "a small or little vine."

The Time and Place. Early summer. Native to eastern North America. (The only other species in the genus is native to eastern Asia.)

The Description. Perennial vine with large, usually shallowly five-lobed, stalked leaves, about as long as wide, to six inches; fruit bluish black, with one seed.

The Virtues. Moonseed is not ordinarily included among the weeds. It usually occurs in woods and along streams. It invaded the fence row in my garden many years ago and persists to this day. As Deam (1940) learned from experience, "when the plant is introduced into cultivated ground, it is almost impossible to exterminate it." Yellow parilla had several medicinal uses among the Cherokee, and some of them were adopted by the European immigrants. It remained a very important medicine into the twentieth century. The fruit, which could be mistaken for a frost grape (*Vitis vulpina*), is poisonous. The grape, however, will generally have more than one seed.

Moraceae Mulberry Family

Mostly woody plants with a milky juice; leaves usually simple and alternate; flowers small, inconspicuous, densely aggregated, usually unisexual. Among the important economic plants, the mulberry family includes the fig (*Ficus carica*) and the breadfruit (*Artocarpus altilis*). Until fairly recently, marijuana or hemp (*Cannabis sativa*) and hops (*Humulus lupulus*) were also placed in this family; they are now in their own family, Cannabaceae.

White Mulberry *Morus alba*

The Names. Mulberry comes to us from the Old English *mor-beri*, which can be traced to the same root as the scientific name. Called white probably because the fruit is nearly white in some cultivated varieties, although it is reddish or purplish in the trees described here. *Morus* is the classical Latin name for this tree; *alba* is Latin for white. Deam (1940) gives the name Russian mulberry, claiming that the Indiana tree was probably introduced from Russia.

The Time and Place. Early summer. From China. (The black mulberry, *Morus rubra*, is native to eastern North America.)

The Description. Usually small trees with slightly milky juice in young stems and leaves; leaves alternate, rather broad, toothed and pointed, unlobed or one- or two-lobed (often all three types on the same plant); flowers small, unisexual (completely male trees, of course, will produce no fruits); fruit berry-like. It is not a true berry as is a blackberry, which is produced by a single flower. The mulberry's berry is a fleshy multiple fruit made up of the ovaries of many individual flowers.

The Virtues. This mulberry is a troublesome weed in my garden for it is hard to eradicate. Birds eat the fruits and often land on my perennial sunflowers, where they may deposit the seeds. The plants that result from them may reach heights of a foot or two before I see them. They can then be cut to the ground, but new

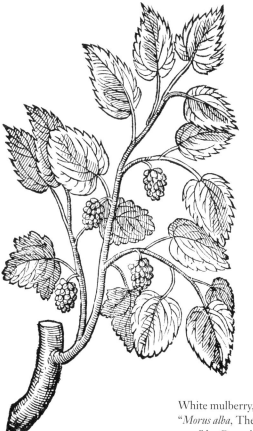

White mulberry, *Morus alba*, called "*Morus alba*, The white Mulberrie tree," by Gerard

plants will arise from the roots. In addition to birds, people often eat the berries. I have had them in both pies and jellies. They are too perishable for marketing but that did not keep my brother and me from picking them and selling them to neighbors when we were children in Bloomington. As I recall, we sold them for ten cents a pint. A wine may be made from the fruits. The Cherokee used an infusion of the bark as a laxative and to check dysentery (which one reader of my manuscript thought a little curious). The plant has its greatest use for medicine in China. The white mulberry was originally planted in the American colonies by the English as food for silkworms, but the silkworm industry failed. Later, they were again introduced as timber for fence posts but did not prove to be good for that purpose. The trees have escaped from cultivation and become successful as weeds or invasive plants in many places in North America. Deam (1940) complains about having to dig fifty to a hundred seedlings from his garden every year because of a neighbor's tree.

Oleaceae Olive Family

Trees or shrubs; leaves usually opposite; flowers symmetrical, usually bisexual, the calyx four-lobed, the petals four, free or united, the stamens two, rarely four, the ovary attached as the same level as sepals and petals. This family includes the olive (*Olea europaea*), which alone would make it very important economically. Other well-known members of the olive family are the jasmines (*Jasminum*), forsythias (*Forsythia*), lilacs (*Syringa*), and ashes (*Fraxinus*).

Privet *Ligustrum vulgare*

The Names. My two dictionaries both say that privet is of unknown origin. *Ligustrum* is the old Latin name for this plant; *vulgare* is Latin for common.

The Time and Place. Early summer. From Europe.

The Description. Deciduous shrub to fifteen feet tall; leaves dark green, one to two and a half inches long, elliptic to ovate, neither hairy nor toothed; calyx four-toothed, corolla deeply four-lobed, white, to a quarter inch long; fruit blackish, berry-like, one- or two-seeded.

The Virtues. To me, privet is *the* hedge plant. I remember it was widely used when I was a boy, and when we bought a new house in 1956 I knew exactly what I wanted to cover that forty feet of space in the back next to the street. Privet was inexpensive, easy to plant, and grows rapidly with little or no care. For many years I trimmed it by hand before finally buying an electric clipper. I don't remember that the plants ever set seed, probably because I nearly always cut off the flowers. I enjoyed the fragrance but my wife hated it. The only annoyance of the plants to me was that they would sometimes send up new shoots three or four feet from the main plant. I did appreciate the privacy the hedge afforded us. (I wasn't going to speculate, but you don't suppose that the name comes from privity, a word one of whose old meanings was privacy?)

When Deam wrote in 1940, he did not include *Ligustrum vulgare* in his *Flora of Indiana*. Although there had been two earlier reports of this species in the state, he couldn't accept them because he had never seen plants that had escaped from cultivation. The previous reports he thought could be explained as relict plants around former habitations. In 1950 Fernald reported privet as long established in open woods from New England to Pennsylvania. Only in 1999 did I find it in my garden, and now it is becoming rather abundant. It is given on the secondary list of invasive species in Indiana (Anonymous, 2000). After being here for many years, why did the plant suddenly become so aggressive? Has a change in the plants, the introduction of a new strain, or a change in the climate been responsible? As this book is about to go to press, I don't have time to search the literature to see if some ecologist has provided an answer to my question.

Onagraceae Evening Primrose Family

Mostly herbs; flowers with separate petals, the stamens as many as or twice as many as the sepals; fruit usually a capsule. The evening primrose family has provided several ornamentals of which I think the fuchsias (*Fuchsia*) are the most exciting.

Evening Primrose *Oenothera biennis*

The Names. Primrose comes from the Latin and means first flower. The name used by itself refers to the genus *Primula*, of another family, the Primulaceae. The modifier is used for this family because the flowers open in the evening. My sources disagree as to the origin of *Oenothera*. Fernald (1950) says that its name was used by Theophrastus for an *Epilobium* (another genus of the family) whereas Bailey tells us that it is said to be Greek, meaning wine-scented, and the name was originally given to some now unknown plant; *biennis*, of course, means biennial.

The Time and Place. Summer. Native to much of North America.

The Description. Biennial, two to five feet tall; leaves alternate, short-stalked, rather narrow; flowers in a terminal spike, the petals four, yellow, one-half to an inch and a half long, the stamens eight, stigmas four-lobed; the capsule four-angled, usually an inch to one and a half inches long.

The Virtues. The common evening primrose, *Oenothera biennis*, was introduced into Europe as an ornamental, although it is less attractive than many other species of the genus. It is now a common weed in many places there. The flowers open in the late evening and are worth watching. One may be rewarded by seeing a hawkmoth pollinate them. The pollen grains are connected by cottony threads and if people brush against the flowers they will find a mass of pollen on themselves. The young roots cooked in two changes of water have a taste like oyster plant (*Tragopogon porrifolius*) or parsnip (*Pastinaca sativa*), or so I have read. The sprouts and roots have sometimes been used in salads. I can't recommend them for food.

Probably the greatest importance of the common evening primrose has been its use in scientific studies because of the peculiar behavior of its chromosomes. Much of that scientific study was carried out at Indiana University under the direction of Ralph E. Cleland. From the time our experimental field was established in 1948 until his death in 1971, Dr. Cleland grew his oenotheras there. Many different species and hybrids were grown over the years, but the only one to persist is *Oenothera biennis*, which was a weed around Bloomington long before Dr. Cleland's study started. I recall that Dr. Cleland never liked me to refer to it as a weed. Perhaps he considered it insulting. The Indians used the plant in medicine and it later found a few uses in England, particularly as an astringent and sedative. There has been renewed interest in the evening primrose because of an oil in the seeds that is claimed to have beneficial effects for a number of conditions. I have seen it on the shelves of a number of local stores. It has also become important for medicines in China (Deng et al., 2001).

Oxalidaceae Wood Sorrel Family

Mostly herbs with alternate or basal, compound (usually in three parts) leaves; flowers with five separate petals and five sepals; fruit usually a capsule. Several species of *Oxalis* are grown as ornamentals for the showy yellow, white, rose, or purple flowers, particularly in hanging baskets. One species, *O. tuberosa*, called oca, is grown for its edible tubers in the Andes. Carambola (*Averrhoa carambola*), a tree native to Asia, is widely grown in the tropics for its edible fruits.

Wood Sorrel *Oxalis corniculata* and *O. stricta*

The Names. Sorrel is from the Old French *surelle* or *sorele*, meaning little acid plant. These plants are usually called wood sorrels to distinguish them from the other sorrels (*Rumex*). *Oxalis* comes from the Greek for sour, probably from the taste of the leaf; *corniculata* comes from the Latin *corniculata*, horned, probably from the seedpod, and *stricta* from the Latin *strictus*, erect, referring to the plant's posture. Sometimes these sorrels are called shamrocks and some have thought that the original shamrock was a sorrel, but it is more likely that shamrock refers to a clover (*Trifolium*). Legend has it that St. Patrick used the three-parted leaf to explain the Holy Trinity. At one time all plants with three leaflets were thought to have magical properties.

The Time and Place. Summer. *Oxalis stricta* is probably native to North America, and *O. corniculata*, probably to the tropics.

The Description. Although it is usually easy to recognize a plant as belonging to the genus *Oxalis* from the yellow flowers and the three leaflets, it is often difficult to distinguish the species. The weeds in my garden are rather small short-lived perennials, or sometimes annuals, seldom more than a few inches high. *Oxalis stricta*, usually an erect plant, spreads by means of creeping underground stems. It lacks stipules and has blunt hairs on the stems. *Oxalis corniculata* is a creeping plant and roots freely from the stems. Moreover, it has stipules and pointed hairs, and sometimes has leaves with a purplish cast.

The Virtues. *Oxalis corniculata* is one of the world's worst weeds (Holm et al., 1977). In addition to being weeds in my garden, both

Wood sorrel, *Oxalis corniculata*, called "*Oxys lutea*, Yellow wood Sorrell," by Gerard

it and *O. stricta* are also annoying weeds in the greenhouse. The acid taste of the leaves provides a pleasant snack and they may be used in salads, but one is cautioned against eating too much of them because of the presence of oxalic acid. The Indians found a few medicinal uses for these wood sorrels. (And see the Epilogue.)

Pedaliaceae Sesame Family

Mostly herbs; leaves simple, opposite (or upper sometimes alternate), with glandular hairs; corolla of five united petals, irregular and somewhat two-lipped, the functional stamens four. Sesame (*Sesamum indicum*) is of the greatest economic importance in the family. The oil from the seeds is an important food in many parts of the world.

Unicorn Plant and Devil's Claw *Proboscidea louisianica* and *P. parviflora*

PLATE 20

The Names. The immature fruit of both species has a single horn or beak, hence unicorn plant. At maturity the horn splits into two parts to make a claw. The claw may attach itself to a passing animal. Cattle in the West have had festering sores result, and more than once the fruit has become attached to my trousers when I am in my garden. Although both common names are used for both species, here I designate *Proboscidea louisianica* as the unicorn plant and *P. parviflora* as devil's claw. *Proboscidea* means snout, again referring to the long beak; *parviflora* means small-flowered, which is not very accurate for the corolla is often two inches or more long, as long or longer than that of *P. louisianica.*

The Time and Place. Summer. The unicorn plant had been reported in Indiana but now is extirpated except in my garden. Devil's claw is native to the southwestern United States and northern Mexico.

The Description. Glandular hairy and somewhat sticky annuals to three feet tall with long-stalked, somewhat heart-shaped leaves to ten inches long; corollas about two inches or more long and wide, whitish, yellow, pink, or lavender, often darker mottled; fruit with fleshy covering, body about three inches and horn one to several inches long, at maturity the fruit becoming a dry, woody structure and the horn separating into two parts, allowing the seeds to disperse.

The Virtues. The young tender pods are used for food either as a vegetable or as pickles and are sometimes cultivated for that purpose. The plants are also grown for their showy flowers and unusual fruits; the latter are often used for ornaments and in other ways in folk art. The Indians found medicinal uses for the plants as well as using them for food, but the most important use

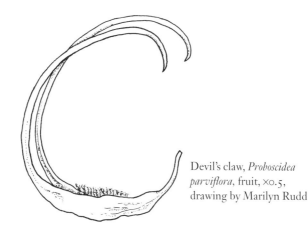

Devil's claw, *Proboscidea parviflora*, fruit, ×0.5, drawing by Marilyn Rudd

of devil's claw (*Proboscidea parviflora*) among some southwestern Indians was in basketry. Bundles of fibers were stripped from the claws of the fruits and employed as binding elements in coiled basketry. As these were stronger than the other fibers used, they improved the durability of the baskets and also served as decoration (Bretting, 1984; Nabhan, 1995). The plant's cultivation led to a domesticated variety that had longer claws and hence longer fibers for basketry. The domesticated variety of devil's claw also has white seeds instead of the dark seeds of the wild type.

In 1976 Peter Bretting began a study of *Proboscidea* for his doctoral research and for several years grew species of the genus at the experimental field. Two of the species have been with us every since. Devil's claw is much more abundant than the unicorn plant, which rather surprises me for the latter is the species that may occur naturally in the Midwest. I consider these species among the most delightful and interesting weeds that we have. My little dog agreed. When I took him to the field with me, he delighted in rolling in these plants (because of the sticky hairs?), much to the consternation of Peter.

Phytolaccaceae Pokeweed Family

Mostly herbs with small, bisexual or unisexual flowers lacking petals; leaves alternate, untoothed.

Pokeweed or Pokeberry *Phytolacca americana*
PLATE 2 I

The Names. Poke is a "perversion of the Indian name" *pocan*, used by Virginian tribes (Millspaugh, 1892). From a museum at the University of Connecticut I learned that poke is *pakon* in Algonkian, meaning a plant used for staining. At one time it was suggested that it was named after President James K. Polk, who used branches of it during his campaign. *Phytolacca* is from the Greek *phyton*, plant; *lacca* is Latin for "crimson-lake" from the color of the juice of the berry.

The Time and Place. Summer. Native to much of North America.

The Description. Tall (to ten feet), stout, often purple-stemmed, smooth, perennial herbs from large roots with broadly lance-shaped leaves; flower with five white or pinkish sepals, ten styles, and ten stamens; fruits fleshy, stalked in an elongate arrangement, dark purple with five to twelve seeds.

The Virtues. Various parts of pokeweed were used medicinally by the Indians, and later the European settlers adopted it for the treatment of skin diseases, cancer, and as an emetic. Deam (1940) tells us that the dried berries were once macerated with whiskey as a treatment of rheumatism, and I suppose that some people found that the treatment worked well without the berries. The berries also at one time were used to add color to wine, but this was discontinued after it was found that they changed the taste. In spite of the fact that the root is deadly poisonous and many authorities recommend that no part of the plant be eaten, the young shoots have long been, and still are, considered one of the best of our wild plant foods, equal to or superior to asparagus. In the spring, shoots appear in farmer's markets. I had heard that the berries were poisonous, but when I visited the Deams in 1949, I was served a pie made of them. Deam (1940) thought that the fruits would eventually have horticultural significance but so far as I know they still haven't. The bitter flavor of the berries can be eliminated by adding vinegar when cooking. I found Mrs. Deam's pie quite tasty but I thought the large seeds were undesirable.

Sometime later, when taking a group of students on a field trip and coming across a pokeweed, I told them that they had probably heard that this plant was poisonous as I boldly put a berry in my mouth. I was swallowing it before I remembered that the berries I had eaten at the Deams' were cooked whereas this one was raw! I died, of course. I read a column in the local newspaper, the Bloomington *Herald-Telephone* (May 7, 1995), that said a tea made from the berries was used by Indians for arthritis, but "this plant is poisonous and its berries should never be used for any purpose." Now they tell me.

Plantaginaceae Plantain Family

Mostly stemless herbs, hence all the leaves generally forming a basal rosette; flowers small, with four sepals and four petals, the latter united, dry, and membranaceous, arranged in spikes or heads. The seeds of psyllium (*Plantago psyllium*) have long been used as a laxative for when ingested they absorb water and increase the bulk of food, thus hastening elimination.

American Plantain and English Plantain or Ribgrass
Plantago rugelii and *P. lanceolata*

The Names. *Plantago* is from the Latin *planta*, footprint or sole of the foot, because of the shape of the leaf of some species. The colloquial name is from the same source. The name plantain is also used for a number of plants belonging to other families.

The name ribgrass comes from the prominent ridges on the leaf. English plantain or ribgrass (*Plantago lanceolata*) is also known as buckhorn for reasons I have yet to fathom. *Rugelii* refers to its discoverer, Ferdinand Rugel, a German botanist who moved to the United States and made important early collections in the Southeast; *lanceolata* is Latin for the lance-shaped leaves.

The Time and Place. Summer. *Plantago rugelii* is native to eastern North America, and *P. lanceolata* is from Eurasia.

The Description. Easily recognized plants: the family description should serve. The flowering spikes of the American plantain are slender and longer than their stalks and the flowers are loosely arranged whereas in the English plantain the dense, thick, often almost head-like spikes are shorter than the stalks.

The Virtues. The first time I saw these plants I thought they were monocots because of the prominent parallel veins on the leaf. I was taught that they are exclusively wind-pollinated but on several occasions I have seen honeybees visit the flowers of English plantain. The plantains are some of the worst weeds in lawns. From the plant's standpoint they are ideal weeds, for a lawn mower will go over them without touching the leaves. My grandmother used American plantain as one of the ingredients in spring greens, but as Fernald and Kinsey (1958) point out for the common plantain, the leaf fibers are too tough to make it agreeable, "otherwise it would not be so common." The seeds are eaten by birds and were at one time by humans, for they were found in the stomach of Tollund man (see p. 116). The plantains had a number of uses in medicine in Europe and were also so used by the Indians.

For a long time I thought that our common broad-leaved

plantain in Indiana (*Plantago rugelii*) was the common plantain (*P. major*), which is native to Europe and a weed in many parts of North America. That species, however, has capsules with lids coming off near the middle and containing six to twenty seeds whereas the American plantain has the lids coming off near the base and containing only two to nine seeds. The latter can also often be recognized by its reddish color at the base of the leaf

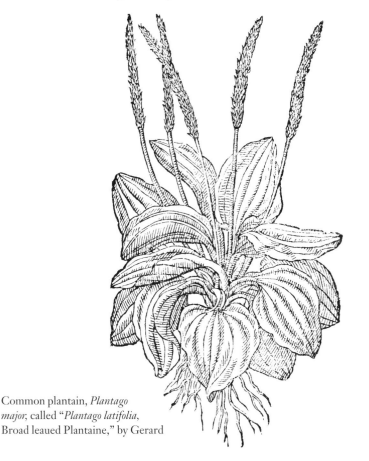

Common plantain, *Plantago major*, called "*Plantago latifolia*, Broad leaued Plantaine*," by Gerard

stalk, which is lacking in the common plantain. Both the English plantain (*P. lanceolata*) and the common plantain are among the world's worst weeds (Holm et al., 1977).

Poaceae Grass Family

Flowers inconspicuous, lacking petals and sepals and consisting of three stamens and an ovary that develops into a single-seeded fruit, the seed-like grain; flowers subtended by bracts and aggregated into clusters known as spikelets; leaves with elongate, narrow blades, sheathing the stem at the base, the sheath splitting lengthwise; wind-pollinated.

The large family Poaceae, or Gramineae, is of the greatest importance to humankind. All the cereals or grains belong here. In addition to rice, wheat, corn or maize, milo or sorghum, oats, barley, and rye, it includes a number of lesser known ones. Sugarcane furnishes most of our sugar. Bamboos, most versatile plants, are important for construction and in many other ways, particularly in the tropics. Our lawn grasses and most of our forage plants come from this family. Grasses are better than other plants in preventing soil erosion in that they often provide a complete covering of the ground and form a mat so the water rolls over them.

A number of plants, including several weeds, that are not members of the grass family may have the word grass in their names, for which I am sorry but there is nothing I can do about it. These false grasses can usually be distinguished from the true grasses by the characteristics given above.

My students in the flowering plants courses frequently mistook some sedges (family Cyperaceae) and rushes (family Juncaceae) for grasses, at least at the beginning of the course. The rushes may be distinguished from the grasses by the flowers, which do have sepals and petals, both three in number, although they are quite small and not colorful. Moreover, they have a capsular fruit with three to many seeds. Sedges often have stems that are somewhat triangular in contrast to the more or less round stems of grasses, and the leaf sheath at the base of the blade is continuous around the stem whereas that of grasses is split lengthwise. Sedges often grow in wetter soils than most grasses.

For the grasses I depart from my usual treatment and give only a very brief description of each. For the identification of grasses, one usually has to resort to technical terminology. Moreover, identification is best done by examining them under a dissecting microscope. In addition to the weeds I include, both red top (*Agrostis gigantea*) and orchard grass (*Dactylis glomerata*) occur in my garden, but they were originally planted and have spread naturally.

Chess or Cheat, Hairy Chess, and Downy Chess
Bromus secalinus, B. commutatus, and *B. tectorum*

The Names. From the *Oxford English Dictionary* I learn that the name cheat was given to these grasses because of their resemblance to certain cereals with which they grow. Therefore, I conclude that they are fraudulent grains, or cheats. Why chess? I do not know, although I suspect it may be a variant of the word cheat. All these grasses are sometimes called brome or brome grass, although these names are usually reserved for the perennial species. *Bromus*, from *broma*, food, is an old name for oats; *secalinus* (chess or cheat) translates as rye-like, *commutatus* (hairy chess) as variable, and *tectorum* (downy chess) as "of roofs," from its growing in thatched roofs.

The Time and Place. Late spring and early summer. All three species from Europe.

The Description. Medium-sized annuals. Two of the species, *Bromus commutatus* and *B. tectorum*, as the names indicate, are hairy or downy. The bracts next to the grains are provided with awns that function in dispersal.

The Virtues. Some species of brome are grown for forage but these three grow only as weeds. At one time it was thought that the weedy bromes represented degenerated wheat.

Crabgrass *Digitaria ischaemum* and *D. sanguinalis*

The Names. Crabgrass was used as an alternate name for glasswort (*Salicornia europaea*) by Gerard and has also been used for knotweed (*Polygonum aviculare*) in England. England is too cool for crabgrasses so likely they were unknown to Gerard. How, why, and when crab became attached to grass I do not know. In vain, I turned to an old scientific monograph of the genus *Digitaria;* the common name isn't even mentioned. I had a neighbor who took great pride in his lawn, and I know that he was always crabby when he found crabgrass in his lawn. He let me know, for the seed probably came from my yard. Spencer's (1957) explanation is better than mine: "The grass evidently got its name because its branching head reminded someone of a crab with its many legs." Perhaps—but I am still not convinced. The other crabgrass (*S. europaea*) was so called because crabs were thought to eat it. *Digitaria* comes from *digitus*, a finger, referring to the arrangement of the flowering stalks; these may be five in number, but more often they are more or less. *Sanguinalis* means "to stanch the flow of blood," from its supposed styptic properties; *ischaemum* is apparently from a Greek word that has the same meaning as *sanguinalis*.

The Time and Place. Late summer into fall. *Digitaria ischaemum* is native to Eurasia, and *D. sanguinalis*, to Europe.

The Description. Low annuals. *Digitaria ischaemum*, which has leaves without hairs, is sometimes called smooth crabgrass; it is semierect and seldom roots at the joints whereas *D. sanguinalis*, northern crabgrass (though both species are found throughout most of North America), has some hairs on the leaves, is decumbent or prostrate, and readily roots at the joints. The two species also differ in their fruits; those of smooth crabgrass are dark brown or black and nearly one-eighth inch long whereas those of northern crabgrass are light gray and slightly longer.

The Virtues. Although I recall having seen both species of crabgrass in my garden, in recent years only *Digitaria sanguinalis* occurs there and is the most abundant weed. It is also one of the world's worst weeds (Holm et al., 1977). Its prolific seed production contributes greatly to its success. The fruits have no special means of dispersal but they get around quite well. On a wet morning in late summer, a short walk in the garden always results in an abundance of seeds on my shoes. The plant's ability to root at the joints (nodes) also contributes to its weediness.

Crabgrass is one of the most obnoxious lawn weeds. I remember many years ago seeing articles in the gardening sections of the newspaper every spring telling people how to control it. Today I rarely see it mentioned, probably because now there are better lawn grasses that compete with it, as well as better control measures. When I lived in St. Louis in the 1940s, crabgrass was the only vegetation in many yards. Mowed regularly it made a good lawn for the hot summer months, but being an annual, it died with the first hard frost and one was left with a barren yard for the winter and spring. If the flower stalks are allowed to develop it also has an objectionable appearance in the summer.

Probably the chief virtue of crabgrass is that it is quite palatable to livestock and makes a valuable forage, although it is not deliberately planted for the purpose. As indicated by the specific epithets, the species were at one time used in medicine. Two other species, *Digitaria exilis* and *D. iburua*, are grown for their seeds for human food in Africa and are known as fonio.

Barnyard Grass *Echinochloa crus-galli*

The Names. It has been many years since I have been in a barnyard but I do recall seeing this grass there so I suppose it is appropriately named. The awns in the flowering and fruiting stalks are responsible for the genus name—from *echinos*, sea urchin, and *chloa*, grass—and the specific epithet—*crus-galli*, "spur of the cock." This grass is not limited to barnyards, of course, and it may at times lack awns.

The Time and Place. Summer. From the Old World.

The Description. An annual, usually two to three feet tall.

The Virtues. A variety of barnyard grass, known as Japanese barnyard millet and million dollar plant, is cultivated as both a grain and forage plant. The grain of the weed was used for food by American Indians, and the plant was also used as a ceremonial emetic by them.

Quack Grass, Couch Grass, Quitch Grass, or Quick Grass *Elymus repens*

The Names. The common names and others—scutch, twitch, and witchgrass—all probably go back to the Old English *cwice*, from the word for lively (for the plant is very difficult to kill). *Elymus* is from the Greek, meaning a kind of grain. Until fairly recently the species was placed in the genus *Agropyron* ("field wheat," hence wild wheat). *Repens* means creeping, referring to the spread of the plant by means of the underground stems.

The Time and Place. Summer. Our weed probably comes from Europe but this grass is also apparently native to gravelly and sandy shores in places in northeastern North America.

The Description. Perennial, one to three feet tall from long, slender, white, underground stems (rhizomes) with dark scales. Even a small piece of the rootstock can give rise to a new plant, which makes it most difficult to eradicate.

The Virtues. To my way of thinking, quack grass is the worst weed in my garden. I have kept it more or less under control by hoeing but I have never been successful in eliminating all of the rootstocks. In 1950 Deam wrote that "most landholders have despaired of ever eradicating it" although some chemical methods were available. Today, with more efficient herbicides, it is still difficult to control, and it is no surprise that it is one of the world's worst weeds (Holm et al., 1977). The plant has had more medicinal use than most grasses. Gerard tells us,

> although . . . Couch-grasse be an vnwelcome guest to fields and gardens, yet his physicke virtues do recompense those hurts; for it openeth the stoppings of the liuer and reines,

without any major heate. . . . Couch-grasse healeth greene wounds. The decoction of the root is good for the kidneys and bladder: it prouoketh vrine gently, and driueth forth grauell. . . . The decoction thereof serueth against griping paines of the belly, and difficultie of making water.

Dogs apparently also have found a medicinal use for it, as an emetic. I have found my dog chewing its leaves at the garden. Another common name for the plant is dog grass. Horses and cattle are said to relish the rhizomes, which are sometimes collected by farmers to feed them. In times of famine the rhizomes have served for human food. One account I read stated that they had a bitter taste, and another said they were sweetish. I tried them and found them rather tasteless, neither sweet nor bitter.

Ryegrass *Lolium perenne*

The Names. Ryegrass was originally raygrass. Ray became rye in the eighteenth century, which sometimes causes confusion for rye is the name of a cereal that belongs to a different genus (*Secale*), and of course it is also a grass. Until recently the annual and perennial forms of ryegrass were considered different species, the annual form or Italian ryegrass going under the name *Lolium multiflorum. Lolium* is an ancient Latin name for this or a similar grass; *perenne*, of course, means perennial.

The Time and Place. Late spring and summer. From Europe.

The Description. Mostly short-lived perennials from one to two feet tall.

The Virtues. Ryegrass is a forage and lawn grass. Although not as desirable for lawns as several other grasses, it has the advantage of germinating fairly readily and is less expensive than blue-grass (*Poa pratensis*) and other desirable lawn grasses. It is often planted with long-lived perennials that can take over as the rye-grass dies out. Another species, *Lolium temulentum*, darnel, one of the world's worst weeds (Holm et al., 1977), which at times is poisonous, is an introduced weed in much of North America but is not yet established in Indiana.

Witchgrass *Panicum capillare*

The Names. I have no idea as to why this grass has the name witchgrass unless the much branched fruiting stalk is thought to resemble a witch's broom. Another, nonweedy species, *Panicum virgatum*, is called switchgrass. *Panicum* is from the Latin *panus*, "an ear of millet"; *capillare* means hair-like, which I also imagine refers to the fruiting stalks.

The Time and Place. Summer. Native to most of North America.

The Description. Annual, two to four feet tall.

The Virtues. Witchgrass is sometimes used in winter bouquets. The slender, much branched seed stalks are rather attractive. Another species, *Panicum miliaceum*, hog millet, broom corn, or proso, is a minor cereal.

Timothy *Phleum pratense*

The Names. This grass was brought from New York to Carolina by Timothy Hanson. It was also called Herd grass, a name now little used, after a Mr. Jonathan Herd, who reportedly found it growing in Pennsylvania. Why some grasses receive the first name of the person who found or introduced it and others receive the last name I do not know. *Phleum* is from the Greek *phleas*, the name of some reed; *pratense* translates as "of meadows."

The Time and Place. Summer. Introduced into the Colonies from England in the early eighteenth century.

The Description. The English name, meadow cattail grass, is very descriptive. The spike-like flowering and fruiting structure, one to several inches long, is not unlike that of some squirrel tail grasses (*Setaria*). Timothy is a perennial, one to three feet tall, with the stems having a bulbous base.

The Virtues. Although perhaps not as important as in earlier years, timothy is still grown as a forage and pasture grass.

Annual Bluegrass *Poa annua*

The Names. Some members of the genus *Poa* have a bluish cast to their foliage, and the name bluegrass is sometimes used for any of the species. This one doesn't have much blue in it. Some books give the name as spear grass. *Poa* is an ancient Greek name for a grass; *annua* is Latin for annual.

The Time and Place. Spring. Native to Eurasia.

The Description. A low annual grass.

The Virtues. I know of none special for *Poa annua*. Kentucky bluegrass (*P. pratensis*), a perennial, is the best-known member of the genus and is one of the most common lawn grasses. It is native to Europe and perhaps also to some of the northern states and Canada, but not to Kentucky. Annual bluegrass is never frequent in my garden, but it is regarded as an invasive species in southern Georgia.

Foxtail or Squirrel Tail *Setaria faberi, S. glauca,* and *S. viridis*

PLATE 22

The Names. Foxtail and squirrel tail are rather descriptive of the flowering and fruiting stalks, particularly of *Setaria faberi,* as is the name bristle grass, which is sometimes used. *Setaria* comes from *seta,* a bristle. *Setaria faberi,* named for the man who discovered it, Rev. Ernst Faber (who collected it in China in the late nineteenth century), is called nodding or giant foxtail, both names descriptive of the seed stalk. *Setaria glauca* ("glaucous," or covered with a whitish bloom) is known as yellow foxtail, and *S. viridis* ("green"), as green foxtail; these two common names refer to the color of the seed stalks.

The Time and Place. Summer. The giant foxtail (*Setaria faberi*) comes from eastern Asia, and *S. glauca* and *S. viridis* from Europe or Eurasia.

The Description. All three are annuals; in my garden, yellow foxtail (*Setaria glauca*) is less than a foot tall, green foxtail (*S. viridis*) one to two feet, and giant foxtail (*S. faberi*) three to four feet. The flower stalk and seed stalk is a spike-like structure with numerous bristles. That of the giant foxtail sometimes reaches eight inches whereas those of the yellow and green foxtails are no more than an inch or two long.

The Virtues. The greatest claim to fame of the foxtails is that one species, foxtail millet (*Setaria italica*), is valued for its grains for food or as a forage grass. It was introduced into the United States as a forage grass and has escaped to become a common weed. It is found in Bloomington and may have been in my garden at one time, but I haven't seen it there in the last three years when I made a deliberate search for it. Green foxtail (*S. viridis*) and bur bristle grass (*S. verticillata*) are among the world's worst weeds (Holm et al., 1977). In spite of its ill repute, I find the green foxtail rather attractive. Years ago when I started gardening I can recall only a few grasses used as ornamentals. Today some are grown for that purpose, proving that a plant doesn't have to have showy flowers or fruits to become appreciated. Some foxtails are cultivated under the name bristle grass. One of the most popular is *S. palmifolia*, often called palm grass, which is native to India.

Johnson Grass *Sorghum halepense*

The Names. Although many species receive their scientific names in honor of people, few common names do. About 1874 this one was named after William Johnson, a farmer in Alabama, who apparently introduced it earlier in that state as a pasture plant. The name Johnson grass is now well established as the common name in the United States but other names, forty of them, in fact, were used earlier, including Means grass. Both Thomas Means and his son John, who became governor of South Carolina, have received credit, probably incorrectly, for the introduction of the plant to the United States. Unlike scientific names, however, the earliest common name is not necessarily accepted because of its priority.

Before the end of the nineteenth century, Johnson grass had a wide distribution in the United States and the difficulty of eradicating it led to the first federal appropriation designed specifically for weed control, in 1900. Johnson grass is still regarded as one of the world's very worst weeds (Holm et al., 1977). I have nothing to indicate whether Mr. Johnson felt honored to have the weed named for him. The most detailed study of the introduction and naming of the plant is by McWhorter (1971).

The Time and Place. Summer. From the Mediterranean area.

The Description. Coarse perennial from rhizomes, three to eight feet tall.

The Virtues. It is difficult to find any virtues for the plant other than the fact that livestock will eat it, for in addition to being one of the very worst weeds and invasive, Johnson grass may at times be poisonous because of the production of prussic acid. Perhaps the grass's greatest claim to fame is that it is related to a species of great economic importance, *Sorghum bicolor*, which includes the grain sorghums, frequently called milo in the United States, the sweet sorghums, used for their syrup, and broom-corn, used for making brooms. *Sorghum bicolor* also includes a weed, known as shatter cane or chicken corn. Once fairly rare in Indiana, it is now extremely common in cornfields. The plant mimics corn (*Zea mays*) until it flowers, but at maturity the dark seed-like grains make it stand out readily. I have grown it in my garden to have material for my class, but fortunately it did not reseed itself there.

Gama Grass *Tripsacum dactyloides*

The Names. One dictionary states that perhaps the common name comes from grama, a name used for pasture grasses in the western states. Weatherwax (1954), an authority on grasses, writes that he did not recall the common name gama grass having been used, but he doesn't explain the name or offer any substitutes for it. *Tripsacum* probably comes from the Greek *tribein*, to rub, "perhaps in allusion to the polished spikelet" according to Fernald (1950); *dactyloides* translates as "with fingers," referring to arrangement of the flowering spikes.

The Time and Place. Summer. Native to the eastern United States.

The Description. Large perennial from three to nine feet tall; flowering spikes with male flowers borne above the female ones; seed-like grain a bony shiny structure, about one-third of an inch long, unusually large for a wild grass.

The Virtues. The gama grasses (*Tripsacum*) make good forage plants. The genus is also of interest in that it is a close relative of corn (*Zea mays*), and at one time it was postulated that it was involved in the origin of that grain. *Tripsacum dactyloides* is not ordinarily considered a weed. It was introduced to the experimental field about 1955 by Paul Weatherwax and his student Lois Farquharson. It has persisted in some places and has also spread to new areas.

Polygonaceae Smartweed Family

Mostly herbs with alternate, simple leaves; flowers small, bisexual or unisexual, greenish or whitish, with two to six petals or sepals, often called tepals. Probably the most distinctive characteristic of the smartweed family is the thin and almost transparent stipules, which form a sheath around the stems. The best-known members grown for food are rhubarb (*Rheum rhabarbarum*) and buckwheat (*Fagopyrum esculentum*). A number of species are also occasionally grown as ornamentals.

Knotweed or Knotgrass *Polygonum aviculare*

The Names. Knot refers to the swollen areas on the stem. In southern Indiana the plant is sometimes called wire grass because of the wire-like nature of the stems, and one who has tried to hoe out the plants knows that the name is an appropriate one. Five other plants are called wire grass, all members of the grass family. *Aviculare* means "pertaining to birds" for birds eat the seeds (fruits).

The Time and Place. Mid- to late summer. Native to both Europe and North America; our weeds apparently come from Europe.

The Description. A small, sprawling or semierect annual to about a foot long; rather narrow bluish green leaves less than one inch long; inconspicuous flowers.

The Virtues. This tough little "annoying weed," as Deam (1940) calls it, has been a weed in my garden since the first year. It has never occurred in large numbers, however, except for one year. An area was plowed for planting in the spring but I didn't get around to it until summer, at which time I found a nearly solid stand of knotgrass. The plant has been much used in folk medicine for a variety of ills, including malaria and cancer. Among other illnesses that it was good for, Gerard tells us,

> the iuyce of Knot-grasse is good against the spitting of bloud, the pissing of bloud, and all other issues or fluxes of bloud, ... It greatly preuaileth against the *Gonorrhea*, . . . being shred and made in tansie with egges and eaten. . . . The herbe boyled in wine and hony cureth the vlcers and inflammations of the secret parts of man or woman, ...

Dioscorides saith that it prouoketh vrine, and helpeth such as do pisse drop after drop, when the vrine is hot and sharpe. It is giuen vnto Swine with good successe, ...

Knotweed, *Polygonum aviculare*, called "*Polygonum mas vulgare*, Common Knot-grasse," by Gerard

Black Bindweed *Polygonum convolvulus*

The Names. A number of climbing plants are called bindweed, and *convolvulus* is an old generic name for climbing plants, many of which are now placed in the morning glory family (Convolvulaceae), to which this bindweed is not related. The fruit is black, but it is the black-green color of the leaf that gives it the name, according to Gerard. I don't detect any black in the leaves of the plant in my garden.

The Time and Place. Summer. From Europe.

The Description. A twining or trailing annual to about five feet high; flowers small, white; leaves heart- or arrowhead-shaped, from four to six inches long; calyx greenish or purplish.

The Virtues. Seeds (fruits) can be eaten. From the contents found in the stomach of Tollund man, we know that it was part of his last meals (see p. 116). Black bindweed has little use in medicine but Gerard states that the juice of the leaves drunken "doth loose and open the bellie exceedingly." The only place I have seen this plant in my garden is on the fence.

Smartweed *Polygonum hydropiper, P. pensylvanicum,* and *P. persicaria*

The Names. Polygonum hydropiper is called common smartweed, smart because it makes the skin smart. Another name used in England is arsesmart or ass smart. The leaves were put into beds to kill fleas and I suppose someone whose nightshirt crept up one night is responsible for the name. It is also called water pepper, a translation of *hydropiper,* for it often grows in wet places and has a very peppery sensation on the skin or tongue. *Poly-*

gonum pensylvanicum is called pinkweed because of the color of the flowers, although they may be white as well. *Polygonum persicaria* is called lady's thumb from the markings on the leaf (which are not present in the plants in my garden). Grigson (1974) informs us that lady, when used in plant names, usually refers to Our Lady, the Virgin Mary. Some American books also give the name heartsease. How this name became transferred to this plant I do not know. It is usually used for the pansy, a violet and unrelated to smartweed. The species epithet, *persicaria*, is also used as a common name. Gerard tells us that this name comes from the resemblance of the leaves to that of the peach (*Persica*).

The Time and Place. Late summer. *Polygonum hydropiper* and *P. persicaria* come from Europe; *P. pensylvanicum* is native to much of North America.

The Description. Annuals, usually branched; leaves relatively narrow, lance-shaped; flowers in terminal, spike-like groupings. Pinkweed is the tallest of the three, at times six feet tall, and has nonfringed leaf sheaths and five pink or white tepals. The other two smartweeds generally are about two feet tall and have fringed leaf sheaths. Water pepper usually has four greenish tepals and a very strong pepper taste. Persicaria has four to six pink or rose petals and often has purple blotches on the leaves.

The Virtues. There are several weedy species of smartweed and I may have had more than three in my garden. In 1999 the only one I encountered was pinkweed. I haven't seen either water pepper or persicaria there for many years; in general, both prefer wetter soils than those generally available there. The leaves of smartweeds are peppery and may be used for seasoning in an emergency, according to Fernald and Kinsey (1958). The two European species have been used in folk medicine for a variety of ailments, and all three were used medicinally by Indians of eastern North America.

Common Sorrel, Field Sorrel, or Sheep Sorrel
Rumex acetosella

The Names. Sorrel means little acid plant. *Rumex* is the classical Latin name; *acetosella* is an old generic name for little sorrel.

The Time and Place. May and June. From Eurasia.

The Description. Perennial from creeping roots, usually about one foot high; leaves lance-shaped with two spreading triangular lobes at the base; male and female flowers borne on separate plants.

The Virtues. This sorrel, not to be confused with the wood sorrels (*Oxalis*), indicates a sour or acid soil, and when it appears in my garden I know that it is time to lime the soil. After we do so, the sorrel disappears for several years. The creeping root of a single plant can give rise to numerous plants, all of which, of course, will be of the same sex. The plants contain oxalates, which are responsible for the acid taste and can be toxic if too much is eaten. Perhaps because of the latter it is not now as important for food as it once was, but it is still used for salads, cooked greens, and soups, particularly in Europe, as well as for a pleasant nibble when in the garden. The plant also had medicinal uses, including a few among the Indians. Jones (1991) gives a good account of its uses.

Curly Dock or Yellow Dock *Rumex crispus*

The Names. Dock is from the Old English *docce*. The curled leaf accounts for curly, and the color of the older plants for yellow. The Latin *crispus* means crisped or curled.

The Time and Place. May and June. From Europe.

The Description. A stout, taprooted perennial to five feet tall; leaves lance-shaped, curled on the margins; fruiting stalks becoming brown with age and bearing many three-winged seeds (fruits).

The Virtues. Curly dock is one of the world's worst weeds (Holm et al., 1977) and in Indiana is "one of our most obnoxious weeds," according to Deam (1940). Nearly every year it appears in my sunflower plots, and I find a sharp hoe is needed to eliminate it—a dull hoe simply bounces off the plant. Moreover, if the upper part of the root remains it will give rise to new plants, so hoeing alone is usually not sufficient to kill it. I recall that this dock is one of the plants whose leaves my grandmother used for spring greens. It is still so used but the presence of oxalates now limits its use for food. It was once official as a medicine and is still a widely used herbal medicine, as a laxative, for diseases of the blood, and as a spring tonic as well as other ways. The Indians also found numerous uses of it in medicine; the root was the part chiefly employed. The fruiting stalks are sometimes used in winter bouquets.

Portulacaceae Purslane Family

Mostly herbs with simple, entire leaves; flowers usually with two sepals, four to six petals, and stamens the same number as the petals or as many as eighteen; fruit usually a capsule; plants often somewhat succulent or fleshy. Several members of the purslane family are grown as ornamentals; perhaps the most widely so is moss rose or rose moss (*Portulaca grandiflora*).

Spring Beauty *Claytonia virginica*

PLATE 23

The Names. What name could be more appropriate for this attractive little plant than spring beauty? As Mrs. Dana (1893) writes, "What flower . . . is so bashful, so pretty, so flushed with rosy shame, so eager to defend its modesty by closing its blushing petals when carried off by the despoiler . . . ." (The flowers close in full sun.) *Claytonia* is in honor of John Clayton, an early American botanist.

The Time and Place. Very early spring. Native to eastern North America.

The Description. Smooth perennials a few inches to nearly a foot tall from solid bulbs (corms); leaves mostly basal, narrow, two to several inches long; stem leaves smaller, usually two, opposite; flowers with two green to purplish sepals, five white to pink petals, and five stamens; fruit a small capsule with a few black seeds.

The Virtues. The chief virtue of this plant is its beauty. Because of the small size of its flowers a single plant is not particularly noteworthy, but when many plants are growing close together, as they frequently do, the effect is very pleasant. The bulbs are properly called corms (which are underground stem tissue) and may be boiled and eaten, and according to Fernald and Kinsey (1958) they taste like chestnuts. The corms may be nearly an inch in diameter but are usually much smaller. Some work may be involved in securing them for they are usually several inches beneath the surface and can't be pulled up with the plant but must be dug up. An infusion of the plant was used as an anti-convulsion medicine for children by the Cherokee, and eating the raw plant supposedly prevented conception permanently.

It is with some misgivings that I include spring beauty as a weed for I think of it as a wildflower as I am sure do most people. The plant will invade lawns, however, and at times may grow along roadsides. I recall noticing it as a lawn weed when I first drove from Bloomington to St. Louis, and for obvious reasons I remember that it was very abundant in Clay City, Illinois.

I became well acquainted with the plant when it served as my class project in a course that I had with Edgar Anderson at Washington University in 1942, and it was then that I learned about its seed dispersal. I brought several plants into the house and placed them in a glass of water on my desk. After measuring the flowers I left them under the lamp. A few hours later I heard little ping sounds. I had no idea what was causing it, but some investigation revealed that as the capsules dried, the seeds were shot out a short distance; it was the landing of the seeds that caused the sound.

Later at Indiana University, *Claytonia virginica* served as Ph.D. material for two of my students. The first was Norman Rothwell, who found that instead of having a constant chromosome number, like most plants, it has many different chromosome numbers. More recently, Jeff Doyle elucidated the evolution of the species with chemical studies. It was he who placed pots of the plants outside the greenhouse at the experimental field, and seeds from these plants have produced a population that has become established there. The prolific seed germination there was rather ironic, for both of my students wanted to grow plants from seeds and it proved very difficult—impossible most of the time.

Purslane or Pursley *Portulaca oleracea*

The Names. *Portulaca* is the old classical name; the meaning is unknown. Purslane and pursley probably stem from the same source as *Portulaca; oleracea* is the word used for edible garden herbs.

The Time and Place. Summer. Generally considered native to southern Asia and probably introduced into North America from Europe.

The Description. Prostrate smooth annual, forming mats, stems fleshy, often purplish red; leaves succulent, about an inch or less long, usually alternate; flowers small, without stalks and with five yellow petals; seeds many, small, black. The flowers open only in the early morning.

The Virtues. Gerard writes, "Rawe Purslane is much vsed in sallades, with oile, salt, and vineger: it cooleth an hot stomacke, and prouoketh appetite; but the nourishment which commeth thereof is little, bad, cold, grosse, and moist . . . ." He also found many medicinal uses, among which, it was good against worms, good for those who have great heat in the stomach, good for the bladder and kidneys, "and allaieth the outragious lust of the body."

The plant was used medicinally in many other ways in Europe, and the Indians also found medicinal uses for it. From Jones (1991) I learned that long ago the plants were sprinkled around the bed to provide protection against evil spirits. But in spite of what Gerard says, it is a potherb for which purslane is best known today. Many people so use it and if they have gardens they will usually have an abundance volunteering. The leaves may be used raw in salads or the whole plant may be cooked. I find the cooked greens to be too slimy for my taste, but with

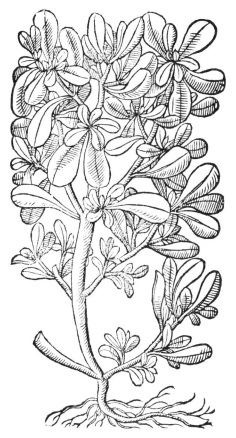

Purslane, *Portulaca oleracea*, called "*Portulaca domestica*, Garden Purslane," by Gerard (Gerard's other drawing of purslane, "*Portulaca silvestris*, "Wilde Purslane," is nearer the weedy type I treat, but I include the drawing of the domesticated type because it is better)

bread crumbs and an egg added they are not bad. In 1992 I saw an item in the newspaper, that studies from the Department of Agriculture in Beltsville, Maryland, indicated that purslane is a rich source of omega-3 fatty acids, which are thought to help prevent heart disease. Herklots (1972) informs us that in the Phoenix Islands of the central Pacific, the people eat as much as two and a half pounds a week. It was also from him that I learned that of the legion of common names, the most graphic is from Malawi, translating as "the buttocks of the wife of a chief," from the fleshy leaves.

Although often rather common in my garden, I don't regard purslane as a bad weed, although it is difficult to eliminate. The root system is shallow and the plants are easily removed with a hoe. If one doesn't remove the hoed plants, they will readily take root again on contact with the soil. Deam (1940) reports that as a boy he pulled it up by the bushel to feed to the hogs. Domesticated forms (as illustrated) are known—one with larger leaves has been cultivated as a potherb, and another with larger flowers as an ornamental.

Ranunculaceae Buttercup Family

Mostly herbs, usually with alternate leaves; flowers with or without petals, when present not united, the stamens many. In addition to a large number of attractive wild plants, some of which are used medicinally, the buttercup family provides us with a large number of ornamentals. Some of the more familiar are anemone (*Anemone*), buttercup (*Ranunculus*), columbine (*Aquilegia*), larkspur (*Delphinium*), and virgin's bower (*Clematis*).

Small-Flowered Buttercup or Small-Flowered Crowfoot
Ranunculus abortivus

The Names. Buttercup comes from the yellow color of the petals and the cup-like shape of the flowers; crowfoot from the leaf shape of some species. *Ranunculus* is Latin for little frog, alluding to the aquatic habitat of many species of the genus; *abortivus* is Latin for abortive and refers to the small size of the flowers.

The Time and Place. Spring. Native to most of North America.

The Description. Annual from six inches to a foot and a half tall; basal leaves roundish, sometimes lobed, stalked; stem leaves unstalked, usually three- or five-divided or -lobed; petals five, light yellow, about an eighth of an inch long, shorter than the reflexed sepals.

The Virtues. *Ranunculus abortivus* is the most unattractive of all the buttercups known to me. It was used among the Cherokee, Fox, and Iroquois for a variety of medicinal purposes.

Rosaceae Rose Family

Herbs, shrubs, and trees with alternate, simple or compound leaves with stipules; flowers with five showy petals, five sepals, and ten to many stamens; fruit various. The Rosaceae are the most important family for temperate zone fruits and include apple (*Malus*), pear (*Pyrus*), almond, apricot, cherry, peach, and plum (*Prunus*), raspberry and blackberry (*Rubus*), and strawberry (*Fragaria*). In addition, the family furnishes us ornamentals: rose, spiraea, cotoneaster, and others.

Mock Strawberry or Indian Strawberry
Duchesnea indica

The Names. The plant looks like a strawberry but the berry is not edible; Indian refers to Asia, not America. The straw in strawberry refers to the chaffy or straw-like little fruits (each containing one seed) on the berry. *Duchesnea* is named for Antoine Nicolas Duchense, who studied strawberries in the eighteenth century.

The Time and Place. Summer. From Asia.

The Description. Rather small perennials, spreading by runners; leaf of three leaflets, about an inch long; petals yellow; berry red, spongy, not juicy.

The Virtues. *Duchesnea* is said to be used as a ground cover or as an ornamental in hanging baskets. This plant appeared in the experimental field about 1975 and has spread into several places, including my yard at home. The uninitiated often think it is a strawberry but the insipid fruit soon dispels that notion. True strawberries have white petals. Neither the fruit of this plant nor that of the strawberry meets the botanical definition of a berry—a fleshy, many-seeded fruit derived from a single ovary—but a tomato does!

Cinquefoil or Sulfur Five-Finger *Potentilla recta*

The Names. Cinquefoil is from the Latin and translates as five fingers, referring to the leaflets. Sulfur refers to the color of the petals. *Potentilla* is from the Latin, meaning powerful, for one European species was considered a strong medicine; *recta* is Latin for upright, referring to the erect habit of the plant.

The Time and Place. Early summer. From Europe.

The Description. Hairy perennial herbs to two feet tall; leaves stalked, with five to seven deeply toothed leaflets, all attached at the same point, and to five inches long; flowers less than one inch across, with five pale yellow, shallowly notched petals and twenty-five to thirty stamens.

The Virtues. Many other species of *Potentilla* are grown as ornamentals, and I find *P. recta* rather attractive. Although a common weed in much of North America, it has always been rare in my garden.

Black Cherry *Prunus serotina*
PLATE 24

The Names. Cherry is from the Middle English *chery*, which apparently came from the French *charise*. Black comes from the color of the fruit. *Prunus* is the old Latin name for plum; *serotina* translates as late-ripening.

The Time and Place. Late spring. Native to eastern North America.

The Description. Trees to a hundred feet tall, bark dark, scaly and roughened; leaves lanceolate, two to six inches long, finely toothed; flowers fifteen to thirty, with short stalks on elongate axes; petals white, about a third to a half inch long; fruit from a third to a half inch thick, one-seeded, the flesh sweet to bitter. The inner bark is said to be aromatic with a rather bitter odor but I failed to detect any odor in some of the trees I examined.

The Virtues. Black cherry has many virtues. Foremost, it has a very fine wood much prized for making cabinets and other furniture and used in other ways. Trees from the forest, now rare, where the competition produces tall, straight trunks, are much preferred to the weedy branched trees from roadsides and other open habitats.

Various parts of the tree, particularly the bark to make infusions, were used as medicine for a number of ailments by the Indians of eastern North America. Its use was adopted by European settlers, and the powdered bark continues to be popular for cough medicines. Nearly all parts of the plant contain hydrocyanic acid, which may be one of the active ingredients in the medicines. On the negative side it must also be mentioned that cyanide poisoning, caused by eating the leaves, has resulted in sickness and death in livestock. Likewise, eating the seeds can cause serious poisoning, even death, in humans, particularly children. I don't find the black cherry as bad in my garden as the mulberry (*Morus alba*) but it is an invasive species in parts of Europe.

The fruits may be used for food or drink; Fernald and Kinsey (1958) inform us that jelly prepared from them is considered one of the finest by many people. From them we also learn that in earlier times the cherries were highly regarded for making "cherry bounce" but that its recipe was not within the scope of their book. I did not feel so limited so I consulted my wife's cookbooks and found a cherry bounce in two of them. The recipes call for cherries or sweet cherries, but it could very well be that the black cherry was once the fruit of choice. The first recipe, from the well-known *Joy of Cooking* by Irma Rombauer (the 1943 edition), calls for six pounds of cherries, five pounds of sugar, and one pint of alcohol; then after five months one pint of distilled water is to be added. In the second recipe, from the *Wise Encyclopedia of Cookery* of 1949, a quart of rum is added to every five pints of mashed cherries. It is allowed to stand "to ripen." How long we are not told, but in the next recipe given, for cherry brandy, we are told that it should be kept for a year as "the flavor improves with age." Cherry bounce, I believe, is hardly something that one can prepare on the spur of the moment for a party. When I find the time, I may try the Wise recipe for I think it should have the greater bounce.

The black cherry was one of the first trees I knew by name. My grandfather had a field with a huge black cherry tree in the middle, and he would always plant corn or some other crop around it. I now wonder why he didn't remove it. Perhaps it was too difficult to do so in the days before tractors were common. Or maybe he considered it a very desirable tree. Many birds came to it for the fruit. I don't recall that my grandparents ever picked the cherries, but it was from that tree that I first tasted the fruit.

The distribution of black cherry extends south to Central America. In Mexico and Guatemala there is a race that has fruits two or three times the size of those of our trees. The larger size, I think, comes from ancient cultivation and selection by people. Called *capulín*, the tree provides a highly esteemed fruit. Shortly after their arrival the Spanish carried the seed to South America, where the tree has done particularly well in the highlands of Ecuador; there, it is called *capulí* (having lost the *n* in its journey). Although I don't recall seeing the tree or the fruits in Mexico, I am well acquainted with the *capulí* in Ecuador, particularly around Ambato where I would frequently see single trees that appeared to be volunteers rather than planted. I never did see orchards of it, but a lot of cherries have to be produced to satisfy the demand in Quito. Often on street corners there I would see vendors, always women, with a large basket of *capulís* and often another basket of *chochos* (*Lupinus mutabilis*). Many laborers in the city would buy a penny's worth from each basket for their lunch—an inexpensive meal and a nutritious one as well, for the latter, a kind of lupini bean, is an excellent source of protein. I found the cherries sweeter than those of our black cherry. The wood of the tree is also much appreciated in Ecuador for it is far superior to the only common tree in the highlands, eucalyptus, another introduction.

Multiflora Rose *Rosa multiflora*

The Names. Rose obviously is taken from the scientific name. *Rosa* is the classical Latin name for the plant; *multiflora* is Latin for many-flowered.

The Time and Place. Summer. An intentional introduction from eastern Asia that has escaped to become a weed or invasive plant.

The Description. Perennial with scrambling stems to nine feet long; leaves with five to eleven pinnately arranged leaflets and toothed stipules; petals white, rarely pink, one-half to an inch long; stamens numerous. The fruiting structure, known as a hip, contains several bony, seed-like fruits.

The Virtues. Sometime before 1940, multiflora rose was recommended in the Midwest as a cover for wildlife, as a food for birds, as a preventative of soil erosion, and as a living fence. The flowers, although rather small for a rose, are produced in great abundance and have a fine fragrance. In spite of these virtues, however, Charles Deam was strongly opposed to its planting, for it became an obnoxious weed and was difficult to eradicate. Although his hatred of the plant isn't mentioned in his *Flora of*

Indiana, he condemned the plant vocally and in letters on many occasions. I first heard of his low opinion of it when I visited him in 1950. In the same year he wrote to Ralph Wilcox, "It makes my mouth sore to talk about multiflora rose"; in 1951 to H. H. Bartlett, "Then this last week another dam[n] thing irritated me. Our State Forester has a million multiflora roses to give away for 'live fences.' I wrote the head of the Department of Conservation he need not worry about a tombstone: he will be remembered O.K. by disseminating this pest all over Indiana"; and to the Wisconsin Department of Conservation, "We have three bushes about a block from here and the jay birds get the hips and fly to our arboretum. . . . Well under these trees I estimate we have over a hundred seedlings. . . . Question is who will dig these pests. The members of the Wildlife Society? No, it will have to be Deam"; and the next year to Daniel Den Uyl, "I understand they are strongly recommending now that all old cemeteries be planted with multiflora rose. When Gabriel sounds his horn I am afraid some will be stranded and not be able to get through the roses. Please do not recommend the multiflora rose except for the bonfire." (See Weatherwax, 1971.)

About 1949, Barbara Shalucha of Indiana University's department of botany established her youth garden next to our experimental field at "Hilltop." Dr. Shalucha decided that multiflora rose would make a wonderful hedge along the roadside leading from the highway to her garden and the field, either unaware of, or ignoring, Deam's comments. The roses did provide a good ground cover, particularly for rabbits, which soon became a problem in her garden, and soon we had unwanted multiflora rose coming up throughout the field, where I am still battling them. I used to take my little dog, Hellfire, to the field and he delighted in chasing the rabbits, even occasionally catching one, but they were always safe when they entered a clump of the rose for no dog would chase after them because of the prickles. After many years a dormitory was erected along the road and a large number of the roses were bulldozed, but some persisted until a few years ago when they were dug out by hand. But they still come up in the field. There are now diseases that are eliminating multiflora rose in the eastern United States (Amrine and Stasny, 1993). I found some diseased plants in 1990 in my garden, but some plants are still persisting and I expect that my battle with them will continue.

Blackberry *Rubus allegheniensis*

The Names. Neither blackberry nor *allegheniensis* require any explanation in the name of the common blackberry, but sow-teat blackberry, which is used by Fernald (1950), does. But unfortunately I never have heard the name used and can offer no explanation for it. *Rubus* is the Latin name for the genus, from *ruber*, red, referring to the color of the berry of some species.

The Time and Place. Early summer. Native to eastern North America.

The Description. Nearly erect, somewhat shrubby perennial, usually five to six feet tall, armed with stout prickles; leaves with five leaflets, rarely three or seven; petals five, white, rapidly falling; berry blackish.

The Virtues. The chief virtue of this blackberry is that the berries are edible and make an excellent cobbler. Nearly every year I pick enough for Dorothy to make at least one. Parts of the plant, particularly the root, were much used in Indian medicine.

Rubiaceae Madder Family

Usually woody plants but our temperate zone ones mostly herbs; leaves opposite, with stipules (or a line connecting the leaves) or whorled; corolla of four or more united petals, the stamens the same number as the corolla lobes. The madder family is mostly tropical and contains two very important economic plants: coffee (*Coffea*) and quinine (*Cinchona*).

Cleavers, Goosegrass, or Bedstraw *Galium aparine*

The Names. Cleavers is from the Old English *clife* and means that which cleaves or sticks. Geese reportedly love to eat the plant, hence the name goosegrass. A number of species of the genus were used to make mats for sleeping, according to some sources, hence the name bedstraw. *Galium* is from the Greek *gala*, milk, for milk is supposedly curdled by some species; *aparine*, an old generic name, means to catch, cling, or seize and is very appropriate (see *The Description*).

The Time and Place. Late spring and early summer. Both native and introduced from Eurasia.

The Description. Weak sprawling annual, stem square with stiff backward-pointing hairs; leaves in whorls of six to eight, one to two inches long, narrow; flowers small, greenish white; fruits of two nearly round parts, to one-fifth inch in diameter, with short stiff hairs. The hairs on the fruit and stem readily allow the fruits and the stems to stick to clothing. Fortunately, the fruits are more readily removed than many bur-like fruits.

The Virtues. The roasted and ground seeds are said to make a good substitute for coffee. The plants, whole, have been used to strain various liquids. *Galium aparine* has been used in medicine, for skin diseases, as a spring tonic to purify the blood, for insomnia, and as a laxative. It was also used medicinally by the Indians. One of its Indian uses was for women to take a bath in an infusion of the plant to have success in love. Gerard gives very few

Cleavers, *Galium aparine*, called "*Aparine*, Goose-grasse or Cleuers," by Gerard

medicinal uses but he concludes by saying, "Women do vsually make pottage of Cleuers with a little mutton and Otemeale, to cause lanknesse, and keep them from fatnesse." Does it work? Even if it doesn't, someone could put it on the market today and probably make a bundle of money.

Scrophulariaceae Figwort Family

Mostly herbs with five petals, united, at least at base, forming a nearly regular to two-lipped corolla, the stamens five or fewer, inserted on the corolla; fruit a many-seeded capsule; leaves various. The figwort family furnishes us a large number of ornamentals; snapdragon (*Antirrhinum majus*) is the best known. The foxgloves (*Digitalis lanata* and *D. purpurea*), from which we obtain the cardiac drug digitalis, also belong to this family.

Mullein or Flannel Plant, and Moth Mullein
Verbascum thapsus and *V. blattaria*

The Names. The name mullein is said by some to come from the Latin *mollis*, soft, referring to the soft hairs; others give the source as *malandrium*, Latin for malanders, which we now know as leprosy, for the plant was once a supposed cure. (I find *malandria* in the Latin dictionary where it is defined as an ailment of horses, as is malanders in modern American dictionaries. More research is in order.) Moth mullein (*Verbascum blattaria*) is so called because the flowers attract moths (although I have never seen any on my plants). *Verbascum* is an ancient Latin name, unexplained according to Fernald (1950), but Grieve (1959) states that "it is considered to be a corruption of *barbascum* from the

Latin *barba* (a beard), in allusion to the shaggy foliage." *Thapsus* comes from the ancient town of that name in North Africa, where it was thought to be native. *Blattaria* pertains to a moth.

The Time and Place. Summer. Both mulleins from Europe.

The Description. Biennials with alternate, stalkless leaves and nearly regular corollas with five stamens. Mullein (*Verbascum thapsus*) is three to six feet tall, with very woolly stems and leaves, and yellow flowers, usually in a single terminal spike-like structure. Moth mullein (*V. blattaria*) is seldom over two feet tall and much less hairy, with white or yellow flowers borne on short stalks. The two species also differ in the nature of the hairs— those of mullein are branched and those of moth mullein are unbranched; to see this, one will need magnification. One doesn't need to see the hair structure in order to distinguish the species, but the branched hairs deserve to be looked at.

The Virtues. Mullein (*Verbascum thapsus*) is a rather striking plant. The first year it produces a large basal rosette, a foot or two across, of long, rather narrow leaves; the second year the flowering stalk appears, more noteworthy for its size and hairiness than for the rather small flowers. It was once grown in England for its beauty, however, and is still offered in some catalogues. A few other species of the genus are grown as plants in the border. Mullein had a number of uses. The downy hairs were once used for lamp wicks, hence the name candlestick plant. The stalks with the flowering end dipped into oil or grease were used as torches, which was cause for another common name, torches. In some places the torches were supposed to drive away evil. An infusion of the flowers was used as a hair dye. At one time nearly all parts of the plant were used as medicine for a variety of ills, and still today some people use it, particularly for pulmonary complaints. A tea made from the leaves is so used. (It is advisable to strain it before drinking in order to remove the irritating hairs.) I have a friend who collects the leaves from my garden to use by smoking for bronchial trouble. Some people have used it

Mullein, *Verbascum thapsus*, called "*Tapsus Barbatus*, Mullein or Higtaper," by Gerard

for diarrhea, perhaps because it may be slightly narcotic. The Cherokee, Iroquois, and Delaware Indians found many medical uses of the plant. Mullein is common in pastures and it is said that livestock will not eat it.

The moth mullein (*Verbascum blattaria*) is not nearly as interesting as mullein, although it may be a more troublesome weed. Few writers give it much attention except Spencer (1957), who tells us that its insignificance is indicated by its having only one colloquial name. He goes on to say that is almost beautiful when it flowers but it is still only a worthless weed. The "greens hunter" may think the basal rosettes of leaves "ought to be good to eat, but they are not."

Speedwell *Veronica arvensis* and *V. peregrina*

The Names. Speedwell is a plant that speeds one well in the sense of prospering or getting well, according to Grigson (1974). My *Random House Dictionary* says that it is so called because its petals fade and fall early. So take your choice. I prefer the former. *Veronica* is named for St. Veronica. *Veronica arvensis* is called corn speedwell; I suppose because it is sometimes found in cornfields. (Corn is the name used for wheat in England or sometimes for any cereal.) *Arvensis* is Latin for "of cultivated ground." *Veronica peregrina* is known as purslane speedwell because of its somewhat fleshy leaves, but much less so than in purslane (*Portulaca oleracea*). *Peregrina* is Latin for wandering.

The Time and Place. Spring and early summer. *Veronica arvensis* comes from Eurasia; *V. peregrina* is native to most of North America.

The Description. Annuals, usually very small, often no more than an inch or two high; calyx deeply four-parted, the corolla four-lobed and slightly irregular, stamens two; fruit a somewhat heart-shaped, flattened capsule with the dried persistent stigma in the notch. Corn speedwell has bluish flowers whereas those of purslane speedwell are whitish.

The Virtues. Some species of *Veronica* are used as potherbs, supposedly as a good prevention of scurvy. Some are used in medicine, both in the Old World and New. One species was used by the Navajo as a charm for catching deer. Speedwells can become weeds in poorly kept lawns. Other species have been cultivated as ornamentals.

Solanaceae Nightshade Family

Herbs, shrubs, and small trees usually with alternate leaves; flowers with five partially to completely united petals bearing the five stamens; fruit a berry or capsule. Our weedy members of the nightshade family have stalked, lance-shaped to oval leaves, generally with toothed margins. Economically, this is a most important family and includes the Irish potato (*Solanum tuberosum*), the tomato (*S. esculentum*), chili peppers (*Capsicum annuum*), tobacco (*Nicotiana tabacum*), a number of drug plants, and many ornamentals, among which the petunia (*Petunia hybrida*) is the best known. The family also includes a large number of poisonous plants. Many years ago I did a little book on the family, *Nightshades: the Paradoxical Plants* (1969).

Jimsonweed, Thorn Apple, or Stinkweed
Datura stramonium
PLATES 25 AND 26

The Names. The English colonists found this plant growing at Jamestown, and the name for this weed later became contracted to Jimson. Thorn apple comes from the spiny outgrowths on the fruit, which is the size of a small apple. Stinkweed, a name that I have heard in Indiana, is most appropriate, for the leaves and stems when bruised have a foul odor. *Datura* is from a Hindustani name for the plant; *stramonium* is an old generic name, probably from *struma*, Latin for swelling.

The Time and Place. Summer. Nativity has been uncertain—some books give Asia but now it seems that Mexico is its homeland. *Datura* has some species native to the Americas and others to Asia.

The Description. Smooth coarse annuals to five feet tall; corollas white, often tinged purplish, to four inches long, opening in the late evening and usually closed during the day; capsule usually with short stout prickles, splitting open at maturity.

The Virtues. At colonial Jamestown some of the soldiers, thinking this was a salad herb, ate it and turned "fools" for several days and had to be protected from harming themselves. A few years ago, inmates at an Indiana prison, who knew that the plant was a hallucinogen, tried it and ended up in the hospital. Luckily, on neither occasion no one died, for the plant is deadly poisonous and can cause a horrible lingering death. The plant contains the alkaloids hyoscine, hyoscyamine, and atropine, and until fairly recently it had important uses in medicine under the name stramonium. At one time it was the principal treatment for asthma and was often used in cigarettes that were smoked for that ailment. The seeds were the part most frequently used and this may help account for its wide distribution as a weed. Gerard knew the plant and wrote,

> The iuyce of Thorne-apples [in other places he used Thorny apples and Thornic-apples] boiled with hogs grease to the form of an vnguent or salue, cureth all in-flammations whatsoeuer, all manners of burings or scald-ings, as well of fire, water, boyling leade, gun-pouder, as that which comes by lightning, and that in very short time, as my self haue found by my dayly practise, to my great credit and profit.

When the flowers open at dusk they are visited by hawkmoths, which are probably their principal pollinators.

Ground-Cherry, Husk-Tomato, or Tomatillo
Physalis philadelphica

The Names. Ground-cherry and husk-tomato are widely used for various species of *Physalis* and are more apt than many collo-quial names—the fruit is the size of a cherry and grows on low plants rather than trees, and the berry is enclosed in husks (the calyx) and is similar in size and shape to a small tomato although the color is not red. Tomatillo is Spanish, meaning little tomato, and is now in wide use for the domesticated form. In many Mex-ican markets, however, it is known as *tomate*, and the plant that most of us know as tomato is called *jitomate*. *Physalis* is from the Greek, meaning bladder, referring to the calyx. Why the French naturalist Lamarck chose the name *philadelphica* for this species is not known; it is native to Mexico. In older books its name is given as *P. ixocarpa* ("glutinous fruited," referring to the somewhat sticky berries).

The Time and Place. Summer. From Mexico.

The Description. Smooth annuals, one to three feet tall; corolla yellow with five brown or black spots near the base, the calyx nearly surrounding the berry; fruit a light green berry, somewhat sticky on the surface.

The Virtues. The berry is edible. Although many species of ground-cherry have rather sweet fruits that are eaten out of hand or used to make preserves, this one is rather bland. The berries, now common in U.S. markets, are used to make the green sauces widely used in Mexican cookery. These sauces are often rather pungent, which results from the addition of chili peppers. The sauces may now be bought in most grocery stores in the United States, either mild (no chilis) or hot from the addition of the peppers. Although I have found one of the perennial species of ground-cherry in my garden from time to time, it has never persisted, but the tomatillo has been most successful. It was first grown there in 1980 by W. Donald Hudson, who selected it as the subject for his doctoral study. He grew both the domesticated and the wild variety, and since that time the wild one and hybrids of it with the domesticate have become well established. Some of the plants have berries hardly larger than a fingernail, and others have fruits two to three times that size. The fruits of both have been a delight to a number of people who eagerly collect the berries in the early fall to make their own green sauces.

Horse Nettle *Solanum carolinense*
<small>PLATES 27 AND 28</small>

The Names. Nettle is an Old English word that was applied to the stinging nettles (*Urtica*) and has also been applied to some spiny plants. Why horse? I don't know.

The Time and Place. Summer. Originally native to the southeastern United States, now widespread in North America.

The Description. Perennial from long, underground rootstock; stems and leaves with star-like hairs (magnification may be needed to see them) and slender prickles; corolla violet to nearly white; berries yellow.

The Virtues. This plant is one of the reasons I don't go barefoot in my garden. The spines (technically they are prickles) are mean and difficult to remove from the hands, as I have found. This alone makes it an obnoxious weed, but more than that it is difficult to eradicate. The underground stems may extend for several feet and upon plowing these are cut into pieces, each one of which is capable of giving rise to a new plant. Horse nettle also reproduces from seed. In spite of these objections I find it, at times, not unattractive because of the showy flowers and clusters of fruits. Although the berries are poisonous, Indians found some use for the plant in medicine.

Black Nightshade or Common Nightshade
Solanum ptychanthum

The Names. Nightshade is from an Old English word whose meaning is uncertain. Perhaps it stems from plants growing in shady places or from the poisonous properties of some of the species of the family. If one eats a berry of the deadly nightshade (*Atropa belladonna*) it could draw the shades of night forever. Black refers to the color of the fruit. Fernald (1950) gives *Solanum* as being unexplained but others derive it from the Latin *solanum*, meaning quieting, from the sedative properties of the berries. When I first learned this plant it was going under the name *Solanum nigrum* ("black") in nearly all books, then it became *S. americanum*, and more recently it is referred to as *S. ptychanthum* ("folded flower" in Greek). All solanums have plaited corollas.

The Time and Place. Summer. Native to eastern North America.

The Description. Annual, one to three feet tall; leaves stalked, with wavy margins or slightly toothed, to five inches long and about half as wide; flowers white, sometimes tinged purplish, about three to six in each cluster; berries shiny black or rarely dark green at maturity, containing a few stone cells, smaller than the seeds.

The Virtues. The plant contains the alkaloid solanine, which is poisonous. This is supposed to decrease to nontoxic amounts in the berries as they mature. I have found the ripe fruits to have a pleasant taste but I've never eaten more than one or two. However, I have found the cooked fruits make an excellent pie. This species is the common nightshade in much of eastern North America, although *Solanum nigrum*, originally from Europe, is also found in some places. Generally, all parts of the plant are somewhat larger than the native species. *Solanum nigrum* is listed as having a number of medicinal uses among the Indians. I think that many of these references are to *S. ptychanthum*. Three of my former students—Jorge Soria, Donald Burton, and Edward Schilling—have made studies of this group of nightshades and have grown many of the species at the experimental field. The only one that has persisted there is *S. ptychanthum*, which is hardly surprising for it is the only species naturally adapted to the area.

Violaceae Violet Family

Our temperate zone members of the family herbs with basal or alternate leaves with stipules; sepals, petals, and stamens five, the flowers irregular, one of the petals provided with a spur or pouch or longer than the others; fruit a capsule with the seeds borne on the outer wall. Many species of *Viola*, including those known as pansies, are cultivated as ornamentals.

Dooryard Violet, Downy Blue Violet, or Common Blue Violet *Viola sororia*

The Names. Violet comes from an old French word which in turn comes from the classical Latin name, *viola*. The plant often grows in dooryards, as it does at our house, and has a downy pubescence and often bluish or purplish flowers. *Sororia* means sisterly, from its resemblance to other species.

The Time and Place. Spring. Native to eastern North America.

The Description. Perennial from a thick underground stem (rhizome), aerial stems lacking; leaves heart-shaped, to five inches wide, prominently toothed; petiole and lower leaf surface often densely short hairy; flowers borne at about the same level as the leaves, the petals violet or blue to nearly white, slightly unequal, the lower one with a spur and the lateral ones bearded; capsule usually purplish.

The Virtues. To include a violet here as a weed is difficult for me but this one is rather aggressive in gardens. I had always thought of violets as being rather shy, retiring flowers. How wrong I was, for they are very promiscuous and hybrids between species are common. Moreover, I learned from Grigson (1955) that the scent of the violet suggested sex and that it was the flower of Aphrodite! Both the leaves and flowers of the European species, particularly the fragrant or English violet (*Viola odorata*), were used in medicine, and several of native American species were so used by Indians.

Gerard tells us that both a syrup of the flowers and sugared flowers were used as medicine, and the latter have come down to us as a candy. Although we eat many stems, roots, leaves, and fruits of plants, very few flowers serve as food. In all fairness, however, I should add that I think that sugared violets are eaten more for the sugar than the flower. Various species of violets have very mucilaginous leaves, somewhat like okra, and have been used in soups in the southern United States. I have meant to try the leaves of this species for that purpose but haven't yet done so. In addition to the normal flowers, *Viola sororia* and other species have a second type of flower borne near the ground, or sometimes underground. These flowers, known as cleistogamous flowers, never open and produce an abundance of seeds by self-pollination.

Vitaceae Grape Family

Mostly woody vines climbing by tendrils, the latter opposite the leaves; leaves palmately veined or composed of leaflets; flowers small, greenish, and readily falling; fruit a berry with few seeds.

The grape as a fruit for wine and for eating makes the Vitaceae an important family economically. The species most widely cultivated is the Old World native, *Vitis vinifera*, the wine grape.

Virginia Creeper, Five-Leaved Ivy, or Woodbine
Parthenocissus quinquefolia
PLATE 29

The Names. This is more often a trailing or creeping plant rather than a climber. *Parthenocissus* is from the Greek *parthenos*, virgin, and *cissos*, ivy. Five-leaved refers to the five leaflets, and ivy comes from an Old English word probably originally used for English ivy (*Hedera helix*), in a different family, but now used for many other plants as well. Woodbine, from the Old English, also and more properly refers to a honeysuckle, *Lonicera periclymenum*, introduced from Europe as an ornamental and now established as a weed in the northeastern United States, and Canada.

The Time and Place. Summer. Native to eastern North America.

The Description. Leaves of five (rarely three or seven) large, toothed leaflets; tendrils terminating in adhesive disks; petals falling separately; berry bluish black.

The Virtues. Sometimes planted as a ground cover or ornamental for its leaves, probably more so in Europe than in the Americas; the leaves often turn red in the fall. The berries are eaten by birds and are suspected of causing poisoning in children. Used in medicine by the Indians. Some people claim that they have trouble distinguishing Virginia creeper from poison ivy (*Toxicodendron radicans*) and the two plants often do grow in similar habitats, but the number of leaflets is usually diagnostic as well as many other characteristics.

Frost Grape *Vitis vulpina*

The Names. Frost probably because the berries become sweet only after frost; grape is from the Old French *grape*, meaning a bunch of grapes. Originally, *grape* was used for the billhook, a knife-like instrument used to cut the bunches of grapes. *Vitis* is the classical Latin name for the grape plant; *vulpina* means foxy.

The Time and Place. Early summer. Native to eastern North America.

The Description. Stout woody vine; leaves unlobed, heart-shaped, toothed, the tendrils without expanded tips; petals separate only at the base and falling as a unit without fully opening; berries shiny black.

The Virtues. Fruits are edible in the winter but they are not one of the better grapes for eating. Frost grape had a number of uses in Indian medicine. Although not ordinarily thought of as a weed, it frequently occurs along fences, as it does in my garden, where it most likely was introduced by birds.

Epilogue

P ARTLY TO CELEBRATE the completion of the manuscript for this book, Dorothy and I took a tour of Sicily in March, 2002. Once there I was reminded that almost anywhere I travel I am rewarded by seeing old friends, weeds that I have become acquainted with in my garden. I saw several of the plants treated in this book, but by far the most abundant plant in flower all over the island was a wood sorrel, a most attractive weed and a new one to me. Our guide, a Sicilian, said that it was called lemon grass because it grew so abundantly in the citrus fields. My wife was pleased that I didn't interrupt to tell her that it wasn't a grass. More than that I didn't ask why it was called lemon grass when it was as abundant in the orange fields as it was in the fields of lemon. I had already decided that it was called lemon because of the lemon color of the petals. Returning home, I discussed the name with my former colleague, Marti Crouch, who suggested that the "lemon" may have come from the taste of the leaves. I have identified the plant as *Oxalis pes-caprae*, the epithet translating as "foot of the goat." (Don't ask. I don't know why Linnaeus chose it. My daughter who keeps goats as pets thought that it might refer to the shape of the leaflets, certainly not the leaves; my own suggestion is that it was so called because the plant went everywhere goats went.) The plant is native to South Africa and is now a weed (the books say "naturalized") in Europe and other places, including Bermuda, Florida, and California. From Bailey (1949) I learned that it is cultivated in the United States, where it is known as Bermuda buttercup. Colloquial names never cease to amaze me. This one is almost as good as Jerusalem artichoke, although I suspect that Bermuda has more meaning than Jerusalem, for I imagine that the plant entered the United States from that island.

Now, with the reader's indulgence for departing even further from my main subject, I would like to tell about another plant that I saw all over Sicily both as a weed and as a cultivated plant. This one was a shrubby or tree-like prickly pear cactus whose name our guide informed us was Indian fig. She also told us that it didn't arrive there until after Columbus's discoveries, but she didn't tell us whether she thought the plant came from India or the Americas. Linnaeus named it *Cactus ficus-indica* in 1753 and tells us (Linné, 1938) why he selected this genus name instead of *Opuntia*—it was a very old name, very well known, not already used, and applied by the Ancients to a thorny plant. *Ficus-indica*, which means fig of India, had been used as the name for the plant by several herbalists in earlier years, and Linnaeus adopted it although he was well aware the plant was from the Americas as are virtually all cacti. The species was transferred in 1768 to *Opuntia*, probably from Opus, a town in Greece, and a name used by Pliny for some plant.

The many-seeded edible fruit is somewhat fig-like. (The true fig, *Ficus carica*, native to the Mediterranean area, is a member of the mulberry family.) The fruit is an important food in the southwestern United States and Mexico, where it is called tuna, and has become so in the Mediterranean region, particularly Sicily, where several cultivated varieties are known. The pads or joints of many prickly pear cacti, including the Indian fig, are also an important vegetable, raw or cooked, in their homeland of Mexico and neighboring areas. I have not seen them sold fresh in the local groceries, but several brands are sold in cans under the name nopalitos. I am rather fond of them.

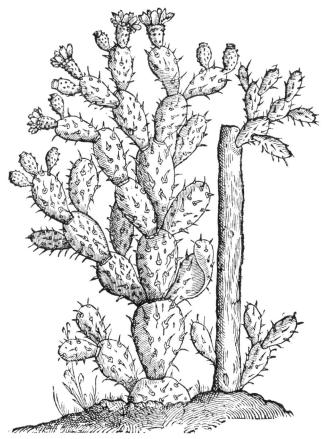

Prickly pear cactus, *Opuntia ficus-indica*, called
"*Ficus Indica*, the Indian Fig tree" by Gerard

The Indian fig has also served as livestock food, more important than related species, because the plants are often spineless, unlike most members of the Cactaceae. The plants have also been used as living fences, but here are sometimes at a disadvantage because they lack spines. It seems only fitting that Gerard, who has figured so prominently in this book, be quoted again in this final passage. He found it a most unusual plant and devoted considerable space to its description, only the first part of which I quote:

> This strange and admirable plant, called *Ficus Indica*,
> seemes to be no other thing than a multiplication of
> leaues, that is, a tree made of leaues, without body or
> boughes; for the leafe set in the ground doth in short
> space take root, and bringeth out of it selfe other leaues,
> from which do grow others one after another, till such
> time as they come to the height of a tree, ...

As to the virtues of the plant he has little to report, nothing from his own knowledge. He had grown it in England but it had never borne fruit, although he had bestowed "great pains and cost in keeping it from the iniury of our cold clymat." He does say,

> we haue heard reported of such who haue eaten liberally
> of the fruit hereof, that it changed their vrine to the color
> of bloud; who at first sight thereof stood in great doubt of
> their life, thinking it had been bloud, whereas it proued
> afterwards by experience to be nothing but the tincture
> or colour the vrine had taken from the iuice of the fruit,
> and that without all hurt or griefe at all.

I have not been able to verify this personally for I do not recall ever having eaten the fruit although I have seen the plant in several places. The fruits also do not appear in our local markets. In my reading I have learned that some species of prickly pear may produce a reddish urine if the fruits are consumed, but I have never seen the Indian fig implicated.

Probably when most people think of cacti they associate them with the deserts of the American Southwest or Mexico. They are not aware that one species, *Opuntia humifusa* ("spreading out over the ground"), the eastern prickly pear, is found in much of the eastern United States.

After my return from Sicily, several people asked me if I brought home seeds of any of the plants. I did not, for several reasons. I already have enough research projects to last a lifetime. Secondly, neither of these plants was producing seeds. I saw no mature fruits on the Indian fig, and the lemon grass seldom, if ever, produces seeds in Europe. Finally, from previous experience I knew that if I brought seeds or plants with me I would have to declare them when I entered the United States.

In spite of the hassles involved in travel today, I look forward to my next trip, to see old friends and make some new ones, both human and plant.

Conversion Table

INCHES	CM		FEET	METERS
0.25	0.6		1	0.3
0.5	1.3		2	0.6
0.75	1.9		3	0.9
1	2.5		4	1.2
2	5.1		5	1.5
3	7.6		6	1.8
4	10		7	2.1
5	13		8	2.4
6	15		9	2.7
7	18		10	3
8	20		20	6
9	23		30	9
10	25		40	12
20	51		50	15
30	76		60	18
40	100		70	21
50	130		80	24
60	150		90	27
70	180		100	30
80	200		200	61
90	230		300	91
100	250		400	120
			500	150
			600	180
			700	210
			800	240
			900	270
			1000	300

References

Amrine, James W., Jr., and Terry A. Stasny. 1993. Biocontrol of multiflora rose, pp. 9–21 in Biological Pollution: the Control and Impact of Invasive Exotic Species. Bill N. McKnight, ed. Indiana Academy of Science, Indianapolis.

Anderson, Edgar. 1939. A classification of weeds and weed-like plants. Science 89: 364–365.

Anderson, Edgar. 1952. Plants, Man and Life. Little, Brown, Boston (reprinted 1997, Missouri Botanical Garden, St. Louis).

Anonymous. 2000. Invasive Plants in Indiana: Their Threat and What *You* Can Do [pamphlet]. Indiana Native Plant and Wild-flower Society, Nashville, Indiana.

Arber, Agnes. 1938. Herbals: Their Origin and Evolution, a Chapter in the History of Botany, 1470–1670, ed. 2. University Press, Cambridge.

Bailey, Liberty H. 1949. Manual of Cultivated Plants Most Commonly Grown in the Continental United States and Canada, ed. 2. Macmillan, New York.

Baker, Herbert G. 1965. Characteristics and modes of origin of weeds, pp. 142–172 in The Genetics of Colonizing Species, Herbert G. Baker and G. Ledyard Stebbins, eds. Academic Press. New York.

Baker, Herbert G. 1991. The continuing evolution of weeds. Economic Botany 45: 445–449.

Banga, Otto. 1976. Carrot, pp. 291–293 in Evolution of Crop Plants, Norman W. Simmonds, ed. Longman, London.

Bretting, Peter. 1984. Folk names and uses for martyniaceous plants. Economic Botany 38: 452–463.

Chandler, R. Frank, Shirley N. Hooper, and M. J. Harvey. 1982. Ethnobotany and phytochemistry of yarrow, *Achillea millefolium*, Compositae. Economic Botany 36: 203–223.

Cocannouer, Joseph A. 1964. Weeds, Guardians of the Soil. Devin-Adair, New York.

Crockett, Lawrence J. 1977. Wildly Successful Plants: a Handbook of North American Weeds. Collier, New York.

Cronk, Quentin C. B., and Janice L. Fuller. 1995. Plant Invaders. Chapman & Hall, London.

Dale, Hugh M. 1974. The biology of Canadian weeds. 5. *Daucus carota*. Canadian Journal of Plant Science 54: 673–685.

Dana, William Starr, Mrs. 1893. How to Know the Wild Flowers: a Guide to the Names, Haunts, and Habits of Our Common Wild Flowers. Scribner, New York.

Deam, Charles C. 1940. Flora of Indiana. Department of Conservation, Indianapolis.

Deng, Yu-cheng, Hui-ming Hua, Jun Li, and Peter Lapinskas. 2001. Studies on the cultivation and uses of evening primrose (*Oenothera* spp.) in China. Economic Botany 55: 83–92.

Duke, James A. 1985. CRC Handbook of Medicinal Herbs. CRC Press, Boca Raton, Florida.

Duke, James A. 1992. Handbook of Edible Weeds. CRC Press, Boca Raton, Florida.

Durant, Mary. 1976. Who Named the Daisy? Who Named the Rose? A Roving Dictionary of North American Wildflowers. Dodd Mead, New York.

Fernald, Merritt L. 1950. Gray's Manual of Botany, ed. 8. American Book Co., New York.

Fernald, Merritt L., and Alfred C. Kinsey. 1958. Edible Wild

Plants of Eastern North America, revised by Reed C. Rollins. Harper & Row, New York.

Gerard, John. 1633. The Herball, or, Generall Historie of Plantes . . . very much enlarged and amended by Thomas Johnson. London (reprinted 1975, Dover, New York).

Gleason, Henry A., and Arthur Cronquist. 1991. Manual of Vascular Plants of Northeastern United States and Adjacent Canada, ed. 2. New York Botanical Garden, Bronx.

Gray, Asa. 1879. The pertinacity and predominance of weeds. American Journal of Science and Arts, ser. 3, 18: 161–168.

Grier, Norman M. 1922. Variation in the flower of the wild carrot. Torreya 22: 64–66.

Grieve, Maud. 1959. A Modern Herbal: the Medicinal, Culinary, Cosmetic and Economic Properties, Cultivation and Folk-Lore of Herbs, Grasses, Fungi, Shrubs & Trees, with All Their Modern Scientific Uses, 2 vols. Hafner, New York.

Grigson, Geoffrey. 1955. The Englishman's Flora. Phoenix House, London.

Grigson, Geoffrey. 1974. A Dictionary of English Plant Names (and Some Products of Plants). Allen Lane, London.

Hardin, James W., and Jay M. Arena. 1969. Human Poisoning from Native and Cultivated Plants. Duke University Press, Durham, North Carolina.

Harlan, Jack R., and Jan M. J. de Wet. 1965. Some thoughts about weeds. Economic Botany 19: 16–24.

Harris, Ben C. 1975. Eat the Weeds, ed. 2. Barre Publishing, Barre, Massachusetts.

Heiser, C. B. 1949. Enigma of the weeds. Frontiers 13: 148–150.

Heiser, C. B. 1950. Weeds are here to stay. Horticulture 28: 363.

Heiser, C. B. 1969. Nightshades: the Paradoxical Plants. W. H. Freeman, San Francisco.

Heiser, C. B. 1976. The Sunflower. University of Oklahoma Press, Norman.

Heiser, C. B. 1979. The Gourd Book. University of Oklahoma Press, Norman.

Heiser, C. B. 1985. Of Plants and People. University of Oklahoma Press, Norman.

Herklots, Geoffrey A. C. 1972. Vegetables in South-East Asia. Allen and Unwin, London.

Holm, LeRoy G., Donald L. Plucknett, Juan V. Pancho, and James P. Herberger. 1977. The World's Worst Weeds: Distribution and Biology. University Press of Hawaii, Honolulu.

Howard, Richard A. 1973. A partial history of the New England Botanical Club. Rhodora 75: 493–516.

Jones, Pamela. 1991. Just Weeds: History, Myths, and Uses. Prentice Hall, New York.

Kartesz, John T., and John W. Thieret. 1991. Common names for vascular plants. Sida 14: 421–434.

Linné, Carl von. 1938. The "Critica Botanica" of Linnaeus. Translated by the late Sir Arthur Hort . . . revised by Miss M. L. Green. Ray Society, London.

Mack, Richard N. 1996. Predicting the identity and fate of plant invaders: emergent and emerging approaches. Biological Conservation 78: 107–121.

McWhorter, C. G. 1971. Introduction and spread of Johnson grass in the United States. Weed Science 19: 496–500.

Millspaugh, Charles F. 1892. Medicinal Plants: an Illustrated and Descriptive Guide to Plants Indigenous to and Naturalized in the United States Which are Used in Medicine. J. C. Yorston, Philadelphia (reprinted 1974, Dover, New York, under the title American Medicinal Plants).

Moerman, Daniel E. 1998. Native American Ethnobotany. Timber Press, Portland, Oregon.

Nabhan, Gary P. 1985. Gathering the Desert. University of Arizona Press, Tucson.

Pickersgill, Barbara. 1981. Biosystematics of crop-weed complexes. Kulturpflanze 29: 377–388.

Proctor, Michael, Peter Yeo, and Andrew Lack. 1996. The Natural History of Pollination. Collins, London; Timber Press, Portland, Oregon.

Randall, John M., and Janet Marinelli, eds. 1996. Invasive Plants. Brooklyn Botanic Garden, Brooklyn.

Riddle, John M., and J. Worth Estes. 1992. Oral contraceptives in ancient and medieval times. American Scientist 80: 226–233.

Salisbury, Edward. J. 1961. Weeds & Aliens. Collins, London.

Silverman, Maida. 1977. A City Herbal: a Guide to the Lore, Legend and Usefulness of 34 Plants That Grow Wild in the City. Knopf, New York.

Smith, Bruce D. 1992. Rivers of Change: Essays on Early Agriculture in Eastern North America. Smithsonian Institution Press, Washington, D.C.

Smith, Bruce D. 1997. The initial domestication of *Cucurbita pepo* in the Americas 10,000 years ago. Science 276: 932–934.

Spencer, Edwin R. 1957. Just Weeds. Scribner, New York (reprinted 1974, Dover, New York, under the title All About Weeds).

Stewart, Doug. 2000. Kudzu: love it—or run. Smithsonian 32(7): 64–70.

Tyler, Varro E. 1993. The Honest Herbal, ed. 3. Pharmaceutical Products Press, Binghamton, New York.

Van der Zweep, Wybo. 1982. Golden words and wisdom about weeds, pp. 61–69 in Biology and Ecology of Weeds, Wolfgang Holzner and Makoto Numata, eds. Junk, The Hague.

Vogel, Virgil J. 1970. American Indian Medicine. University of Oklahoma Press, Norman.

Weatherwax, Paul. 1954. Indian Corn in Old America. Macmillan, New York.

Weatherwax, Paul. 1971. Charles C. Deam: Hoosier botanist. Indiana Magazine of History 67: 197–267.

Yatskievych, Kay. 2000. Field Guide to Indiana Wildflowers. Indiana University Press, Bloomington.

Index